GRASSROOTS TO GREATNESS

THE ULTIMATE GUIDE TO GROWING YOUR SPORTS CLUB

DIPS PATEL

Re think

To Nadiya and Freya, my favourite little people. I hope you will find the joy in team sports as much as I have.

Contents

Introduction

Have you ever wondered why some sports clubs – regardless of their type (grassroots or professional) – seem to win leagues and cups, attract players and get the best sponsors, while your club seems to dawdle along? Why do the best players seem to pass your club by? Why do you struggle to attract volunteers and coaches? Why are other clubs so much more successful than yours?

If you are a coach, a manager of a team, a club chair or a volunteer committee member, you are likely to have experienced stagnation within your club. A lack of direction, a frustration that other clubs have overtaken yours or a feeling that your club culture seems to have disappeared.

The clubs you envy might seem to be the best-run organisations on and off the field, but what is the real secret of their success and how do they sustain it over decades? What is it that makes them better than other clubs? What is their secret sauce?

Is it the people, players or coaches? Is it the culture? The first team? The playing philosophy? The truth is, it's a combination of all the above and more, and in *Grassroots to Greatness* I'm going to unpack these reasons and share them with you.

The role of the sports club in society

Historically, people may have craved the need to meet face to face at the local nightclub, sports club, working men's club or youth club. The digital revolution has changed this and created an insular world. Children, until recent times, would have been seen playing various team sports in streets and parks. Through these 'disorganised' sports, world-class athletes have been created.

This freedom didn't just allow children to play sports, it allowed them to communicate, argue, get up to mischief. I'm sure we all remember playing football on the street, breaking a neighbour's window and running away. The admission of breaking the window and the potential punishment was all part of growing up and learning life skills. Children and young people are now, in the main, preferring to play online, and the role of team sports has fundamentally changed. A sports club is now often the only place a young person can be part of an environment that can give them a sense of belonging, regardless of their age, gender, race or religion.

The role of a sports club within society and its importance has often been overlooked by local councils and governments, and sports clubs had been deprived of government funding globally for many years. Recently, most governments around the world have started to recognise the importance of grassroots sports and increased funding, although the pandemic of 2020 stalled progress in many areas.

We need to make our grassroots sports clubs the home of athletic prowess, alongside giving young people the ability to gain valuable life skills. How can we do that? How can you as a volunteer, with maybe a full-time job and other commitments, do your best with your precious time?

A little about me

During my two decades of working within the sports industry, I've built a base of knowledge as to how to make your sports club successful. I've been fortunate enough to work within a few global sports brands as a global product manager, where I managed the process to outfit national and professional football, cricket, rugby, netball, hockey and aquatic organisations around the world.

I had the opportunity to work across all levels of these professional sports clubs, from the first teams through to the under-fifteens (U15s), with CEOs and specialist coaches. I was lucky to spend quality time with some sporting legends: from Sir Alex Ferguson to the late Sir Bobby Charlton, from Bryan Habana to Brian O'Driscoll, from Sachin Tendulkar to Brian Lara. They all had strong opinions on how sports organisations should be run and I was eager to learn from them.

Meeting these world-class individuals across a variety of sports gave me the understanding of what a successful sports club or organisation should look like. Why did certain clubs win tournaments and leagues consistently, while others with the same resources failed on the pitch? How did behind-the-scenes staff make decisions that impacted on-pitch performances? Who had the final decision? How did other clubs and federations simply not have the resources to get the basics right but were outperforming on the pitch?

Creating a culture of success

It is so important to create an amazing culture and environment in your club as this dictates performance on the pitch or court. Get the culture and environment right and success (be it winning, just having fun or membership increase) will follow. This is the same in business; sports clubs are no different to world-class companies.

If your club is more than twenty-five years old, it's likely you will have some highly passionate (predominantly male) baby boomers who have given a lot of their time to it. They have been the backbone of grassroots sports; some have made the clubhouse their second home. Quite often, their time was taken up on paper-based 'analogue' tasks. Leagues are often run by the same baby boomers, many of them still using these analogue methods. As they start to retire, the next generation will need to take on these organisational tasks in order to keep grassroots sports going. These characters are reducing in number at a rapid rate, be it through ill health, retirement or inability to carry out the tasks they once did. The baby boomers will have to be replaced.

How can you attract and retain the volunteers you need to create a great sports club and maximise their time? How can a volunteer-based organisation become something that is as successful off the pitch as on the pitch? Times have clearly changed, and volunteers are much more precious about their time. If you are going to ask people to volunteer for your club, it is best to have a clear plan and vision for them.

Successful sports clubs tend to be lucky enough to have a broad spectrum of former players and volunteers who uphold the values of the club, alongside being the guardians of the culture. These club members are the support network and mentors of the players who gain success on the pitch. They help guide players through on-field and off-field ups and downs.

The best clubs in the world seem to have an element of magic; an aura of expectation of both players and volunteers; traditions, rituals and methodologies that have been around for many decades. The unique nature of each club's culture is created by its history and traditions, but what if your club doesn't have any? How can you create some?

You need a structure and a formula for success. If your club doesn't have any expectations, *Grassroots to Greatness* will help you create your own culture and vision.

CONSIDER:

- What does success look like? Is it winning every title? Is that realistic?
- Are you an organisation that simply does not have the resources to fulfil the 'winning' desire?
- Do you need to win to be successful?
- Is it OK to accept you won't win the title but being mid-table is your version of successful?
- How is it that teams that often get promoted in their first year end up mid-table but in year two they end up in a relegation battle?

About the book

Part One will broaden your horizons by showing you the most successful sporting organisations in the world and looking at how they answer these questions, how they outperform and what you can learn from them. I hope you can build on some of my learnings and insights so you can start improving your own club on and off the pitch or court.

In Part Two, I'll introduce my 'C + L + U = B' framework (community + leadership + unity = belonging), which will help you identify the areas in your club that need work and create that elusive sense of belonging. Several case studies within the model will help spark ideas to help you develop your club, regardless of sport.

My 'five Ps' framework in Part Three will unpack the pillars that support a successful club: profile, philosophy, partnerships, place and people. This section is full of practical tips and examples.

Throughout the book, you'll be encouraged to monitor your own practice with frequent 'Consider' check-ins. Case studies will demonstrate how both frameworks have been used by hundreds of sports clubs worldwide with clear success rates.

Grassroots to Greatness will help grow your sports club, channel your passion where it is most effective, and engage and inspire local talent and community.

PART ONE
THE GRANDSTAND VIEW

For thousands of years, we as humans have played sport. There is evidence to show ball-based sports were played between 1400 BCE and 400 BCE. Fast forward to the 1600s and this is the first time there is a mention of the team sport cricket in England. A few hundred years later in the 1800s we see lacrosse, football, rugby, cricket, netball, basketball, Australian rules football, and a number of other team sports being formalised. Rules were written, governing bodies were created. We also see the emergence of sports clubs in these times, alongside schools adopting team sports as part of their curriculum. Sports clubs initially were founded as places for people to play sport and socialise in the industrial era. They offered many sports under the same roof, catering for many needs. Fast forward to today, and we have a very different looking club structure. Most grassroots sports clubs globally are single sports clubs, instead of a larger multi-sports club with resources combined.

In this section we are going to explore the differences between a team and a club, and the roles within a club; how to spot if your club has 'healthcare' problems; and, finally, if the structure of your club is the best it can be. We are also going to explore some of the best examples of grassroots to greatness with case studies from the All Blacks and Sir Alex Ferguson.

1
What Is A Sports Club?

A sports club or association is a group of people formed for the purpose of playing sport. Some offer multiple sports, while others are single sports organisations. Sports clubs range from amateur or grassroots through to professional businesses with a global following.

Sports clubs come in all different shapes and sizes. Large amateur clubs can sometimes dwarf the size of professional sports clubs. Some clubs are asset-rich and own their ground and clubhouse, while others are leaner and hire facilities.

Most grassroots clubs have a financial model of members paying an annual fee. Professional (pro) clubs will have higher overheads as they may need to pay some of their players. Pro clubs are likely to have sponsorship fees, revenue for fans, merchandise sales and TV rights.

Team versus club

'Team' and 'club' are often mixed up in sporting language. Many players will say they play for their team, as if the team has no affiliation to the wider club. Supporters will often follow the first team and forget that there might be a larger organisation feeding into it.

Team-first approach

In America, the National Football League (NFL) refers to its thirty-two franchises as teams, not clubs. They do not have a pathway or a feeder system. Why? The NFL uses the college sporting system and high schools to attract the best talent. These colleges and schools develop the players en masse. The franchise philosophy, administration and coaching prioritise winning at all costs in order to gain the revenue to afford better talent the following season, so they do not invest in youth sections or pathways.

Within the English and European sporting system, each club can develop home-grown talent. This means a club-first approach is taken unless a club wants only short-term success. A team-first approach occurs when coaches, captains and managers protect the players within their team, making sure they are not involved with the wider club. This does create team stability, but it doesn't support the development of players and the wider club.

In several clubs I've been involved with, a player will pigeonhole themselves into a certain team and refuse to play if they are dropped to a lower team. I've also experienced the opposite when a player has refused to play up a team, where they were selected on form, performance or the fact there were a number of injuries in the teams above. This behaviour has been tolerated by the club, whereas other clubs would not accept it.

Other examples include when an age group coach says, 'he is my player' or 'he belongs to the third team'. Coaches being protective over their own team can be hugely detrimental to the wider club and the individual player. A team-first manager is likely not to allow their players to move up or down within the club. They want to win at all costs, rather than focus on player development with a longer-term outlook. This team-first approach will, over time, create a dysfunctional club. The club may have needed these players in different age groups, or the player might be better than his or her age group and need to be pushed into the next category.

At my company, KitKing, football managers often contact us to purchase their team's kit. The sales team will ask for the club's home and away colours. Most football clubs have clearly defined home colours for their kits, but away kits can often reveal whether the manager has a club-first or team-first approach. Club-first managers will often highlight the club colours and stick to them, whereas team-first managers will force their own preferences. How do they get away with this? These managers realise that away fixtures are out of the sight of the wider club and therefore feel free to create a new set of colours and a fresh identity for their team.

There are many examples of when sporting organisations end up thinking about their teams rather than their club. The English Cricket Board (ECB) and English Football Association (FA) both recognised that the national side had a long period of failure on the global stage. They realised that coaches being appointed from abroad every few years meant that the playing philosophy was constantly changing. They also saw that there was no pipeline of talent within the FA or ECB. Players selected for the U17s were not likely to feature in the men's first team. As a result, due to short-term selections, the international team was not playing for the wider organisation but were playing as a disorganised team.

I believe that this is why I've never seen the England men's football team lift a trophy in my lifetime, and I didn't witness this for England cricketers until 2005.

Club-first approach

A successful sports club will make sure there is a club-first rather than a team-first approach. Players will get to move around – those in the first team are likely to train with second team and academy players. With a club-first approach it's likely that the seniors will support the 'feeder' teams, either by their presence at key fixtures or potentially by coaching the future stars. In the event senior players are injured, they are likely to be dropped and play lower down the club to regain their spot in the more senior team. A club-first approach has been proven time and time again to be the most successful way of running a sporting organisation.

In 2000, the ECB created a National Academy (now the National Cricket Performance Centre) based at Loughborough University as the 'home' of team England, for the full set of age groups. It was strategically located, being central in the country – a maximum of three hours away from 90% of the population. A director was appointed and a playing philosophy created, and within five years England lifted the Ashes.

The FA have had a similar story in that decades of poor performances at the Euros and the World Cup (no wins since 1966) resulted in a rethink and a reset in 2013. The FA started to think about 'team England'. They reflected on the frequent changes to playing philosophy and the lack of an England football pathway for players and coaches. Finally, there was no base for team England that all the different teams could call their 'clubhouse'.

Greg Dyke laid out a set of targets that many thought were unachievable. He recognised that there was a 'team England' but no sense of a 'club England'. Players and coaches would come and go and wouldn't know about the wider organisation.

It all started in 2012 when the FA created a home for 'club England' at St George's Park. Greg Dyke set out a plan to create an England DNA that would run throughout every representative side, male or female. It would mean that players could move through the age groups, having a set of expectations and consistency. The playing philosophy would not change, with the same brand of football throughout the organisation. The FA researched other successful national teams and recognised that success at a youth team level directly correlated to success at the men's team level. In 2017, England won the U17s World Cup. More recently, the women's side won the 2022 Euros and claimed silver in the 2023 World Cup.

There are many other examples of a club-first approach: Barcelona, Manchester United under Sir Alex Ferguson, and the All Blacks. Each has a specific brand of how they play. Players train together over many hours in the same style and format. This results in consistency of selection and player expectation, and results in a higher win rate than other clubs. When players are injured or need to be replaced, a player further down the pathway is ready to step into that role, with a consistent playing style and philosophy enabling a smooth transition.

This thinking has started to become broader than just playing. What happens when a coach, senior player or captain retires? We are starting to see many clubs retain them in either coaching or ambassador-type roles. A seventeen- or eighteen-year-old having the ability to rub shoulders with a player whom they idolise or who has played in their position and was successful has clear benefits for the club.

The multi-sports legacy

Globally, you can trace the origin of established sports clubs back to the British. Sports clubs around the world are more likely to be multi-sports clubs; however, in the UK they are more likely to be single sports clubs.

Why does multi-sports make a difference? Historically, a club that is asset-rich, ie that owns its land and playing field, would have to commercially maximise the use of its ground and clubhouse. This, in turn, results in more people using the ground and facilities, therefore its membership base becomes a lot wider. Less-popular sports such as squash or hockey would be tagged on to larger sports. Overall, these clubs tended to be 'super clubs', if they were managed properly.

Examples of multi-sports clubs

Did you know Italian football giant AC Milan was originally named Milan Football & Cricket Club? Englishmen Herbert Kilpin and Samuel Davies founded the club, which has retained is anglicised name of Milan (rather than Milano) out of respect for their English roots.

FC Barcelona might now be known for their dominance in Spanish and European football; however, they field teams in five other sports: basketball, handball, futsal, roller hockey, and more recently we have seen a FC Barcelona eSports section being launched.

Another example of a multi-sports club is Hong Kong Cricket Club (HKCC). In June 1851 a public meeting was held where it was proposed that a turf playing ground would be built on the waterfront to become the birthplace of one of the first cricket clubs outside of England. Shortly after, HKCC was formed, with the purpose of promoting the games of cricket, tennis, croquet and other athletic sports. Today, the club has outstanding facilities for hockey, swimming, golf, lawn bowls, netball, squash, table tennis and snooker as part of the overall club.

The global legacy of multi-sports clubs is not widely replicated in the UK, where single sports clubs are more common. A great example of a sports town is Billericay in Essex. Billericay Town FC, Billericay Lawn Tennis Club and Billericay Cricket Club are all located on the same site in the town but run independently as standalone legal entities. There are also St Johns Billericay Cricket Club and Billericay Rugby Football Club on the other side of town.

Summary

The team-first approach is standard in the US, where teams focus exclusively on winning rather than developing future talent. In the UK and Europe, the club-first model is favoured. The success of such an approach has been seen in England cricket and football, where consistent 'club' expectations and playing philosophy has led to a successful period of performance for all representative sides.

CONSIDER:

- Do you have a club-first approach?
- Do you have a club DNA?
- Does your club have a coaching and player pathway?

2

Your Club's Health Check: What Are The Key Problems?

It's easy to find the negative aspects of your club, be it individuals, facilities or a lack of resources. I've seen clubs use their lack of resources as an excuse for their failures to grow junior sections or blame a lack of money for their failure to start up a women's and girls' section. Negativity breeds negative energy, which seeps out through the pores of the club and gets passed on to staff, volunteers, coaches and, in turn, players.

Every club has its limitations, be it a poor clubhouse or pitches or a lack of juniors', women's or girls' sections. Ultimately, it is the leadership group's job to create positivity within the committee, which in turn will filter through to different areas of the club.

Here is a list of the most common problems sports clubs face:

- Recruitment and/or retention of volunteers, members and coaches

- Recruitment and/or retention of youth section players

- Lack of finances to run the club

- Change in demographic within the catchment area

- Pitch or court availability and cost

- Poor standards of pitches, courts or general facilities

- Members, players and coaches unclear on the overall club purpose, vision, expectations and ambition

The first step in solving any problem is to admit there is one. Far too often, the leadership group within a club does not admit to any difficulties, but once a problem has been identified, solutions can be found.

Throughout this book we'll work at addressing and eliminating the problems listed above. We'll make a start here and suggest other early warning signs that your club might be in trouble.

Recruitment and/or retention of volunteers, members and coaches

Here are some ideas to help resolve the problem of recruiting and retaining volunteers, members and coaches.

Partner with educational institutions

Local colleges, schools and universities will all have young coaches that need to complete coaching hours in order to pass their courses. It's imperative to make sure your coaches are passionate about people development, not just dads doing it to 'help out' from a sense of duty. If you need to pay your coaches, do it.

Build a pipeline of talent (grow your own coaches)

By creating a young leadership programme and allowing the juniors in the club to take on leadership roles, not only does it mean you have 'coaches in waiting' but you also develop young players' ability to have a leadership role with some responsibility within the club. Some clubs will brand this scheme as a young leadership programme, while other clubs are not as formal and the expectations are just for teenagers to support younger club members.

Invest in parents

Parents are a great source of coaching talent, if used in the right way. Parents often watch on the sidelines throughout training sessions, but I'm a big fan of getting them involved. If you ask parents to take coaching qualifications they will often say no at first. However, if you get them involved over a period of time they will feel more confident to achieve these.

The expectations of parents who coach must be clear, especially regarding how they should treat their own child. The leadership group is responsible for defining these expectations.

What other ways can parents support the club? What skills can they bring from their day jobs? For example, the club might be short of a treasurer and it's often left to the playing adult sides to fill a gap, but there might be a parent with the necessary skills who could take on the role.

Recruitment and/or retention of youth section players

The following ideas will help you recruit a strong junior team.

Enjoyment is key

Junior retention is a critical factor for a successful club. A lack of juniors means a lack of pipeline talent. We've given some attention to the pipeline above, but I should add that if juniors have a structured and organised training regime with inspirational coaches, they are going to enjoy themselves and share their enjoyment with their friends. Word of mouth will spread.

If juniors are not enjoying themselves, the question is, why not? What is it about the programme that is a problem? It is the leadership team's responsibility to solve it. Common problems include coaches that are not making training enjoyable or facilities that are not available during reasonable hours. If players leave, make sure you find out why. Keep in touch, as once you have solved the problem you may find they will return.

Attract the best players through schools, colleges and universities

Partnering with local schools, colleges and universities is an easy win. Build deep and meaningful relationships with these institutions. Identify and build a rapport with the key stakeholders within each one. Once you have a few players come through, more will follow. Make sure that you keep in contact and don't come across as a club that just wants to take, with nothing to give in return.

Invite schools, colleges and universities to an annual open day for potential players to meet the key members of the club. Creating a flyer via online software such as Canva (www.canva.com) can be an impactful method of getting potential players along to your club. Ideally, run the event when the weather is great, ie in summer.

Find a way of sharing the club's playing philosophy by engaging potentially new players in an interactive way. The open day is not just for established players or teenagers with potential; use it to build your pipeline of talent. Getting local primary schools to market this day for you will result in young players joining your junior section.

The open day is also a great opportunity to invite local businesses to advertise and support your club.

Lack of finances to run the club

Coaches are the Pied Pipers of the club – they attract players. High-quality coaching sessions that challenge players at all levels deserve incentives and rewards.

The better the standard of coaching, the more likely players are going to improve. The more players improve, the more fun they will have. The more fun players have, the more likely they are to bring that positive energy into a game and win. The more they win, the more players you will attract and retain.

It is not always possible to pay, but is there a way you could financially reward coaches without exchanging cash? Something that might be of low value to the club but high value to the coach? This could be in the form of free kit, a drink behind the bar or, if the coach is a player, you could waive the annual subs.

Change in demographic within the catchment area

Think outside the box regarding player recruitment; establishing links with local groups and communities is one way to approach this.

Have you explored all recruitment options and dived into all pockets of the local community that may hold talent? A great example could be local churches, mosques, temples or synagogues, or local refugee groups.

Many sports have a reputation for not accepting those of different faiths, cultures and beliefs. Times have changed, and the majority of sports clubs now recognise the need for diversity, but clubs often are yet to established links with local groups that might be outside of their comfort zone.

CONSIDER:

- Is there a local temple or mosque you could reach out to?
- Could you contact a local Scout or Guide group?

Pitch or court availability and cost

If a club is not fortunate enough to own its own pitch or court, then it's likely that pitch/court hire will be one of its biggest costs. Equally, once a club does find an available pitch or court to hire, availability then becomes a huge problem. There is no easy solution, so learn to think outside the box and like an entrepreneur.

I've heard of established clubs with pitches being approached by start-up clubs to hire their facilities on days that the club is not playing or training. More often than not, the request will go to the leadership group of the club and get rejected.

We are naturally protective over our turf, but there are some good reasons to allow a start-up club to hire facilities. The established club would gain a new revenue stream that would potentially help to upgrade its own facilities, and it may end up attracting some of their players. Far too often, leadership groups are not collaborative enough and end up missing opportunities to enhance their club.

CONSIDER:

- Are there any facilities that are available that are not in use, eg within a school, college or university?
- Could you potentially partner with an existing club that might not use their pitch on certain days?

Poor standards of pitches, courts or general facilities

Average clubs are often awful at maintaining their environment, allowing the maintenance of the club to drift.

Making a club environment welcoming and attractive will naturally attract volunteers, members and coaches.

CONSIDER:

- Is the club clean?
- Do you have facilities for all genders and demographics?
- Is the club fully inclusive?

Members, players and coaches unclear on the overall club purpose, vision, expectations and ambition

You are what Google says you are. Far too often, clubs don't focus on their digital presence. Kit and identity is also such an important part of player recruitment, it shouldn't be underestimated.

Websites and social media

Imagine a scenario: England lift the World Cup and a little boy or girl says they are inspired to play. What is mum or dad likely to do? Get out their phone and do a quick search on Google or social media platforms.

Getting your website and social media accounts up, running and to a high standard is critical. Try to find a volunteer that has the skills and time to maintain the various platforms. If you don't have anyone within the club to build your website, it's a worthwhile investment to employ a freelancer or local agency to do the initial build. Once built, then transfer over to volunteers who can share the responsibility of maintaining the site.

I'd always recommend that a committee creates an annual calendar of activity. This will show when your social media pages and websites will need their frequent updates and when you will need administrative resources.

If you don't have a smart website, what does that say about your club? Many clubs use their website to communicate with themselves and forget that it is the shop window to inspire potential new talent or juniors to play.

Kit and identity

You have now attracted a young and talented player to join your club. He or she may have the choice of your club over another. Your club doesn't have a strong kit offering, but the other club does. Your club doesn't have a solid set of colours or expectations of what to wear for training, while the other club has a strict set of expectations regarding what to wear and how to present yourself. Which do you think the player will choose?

Having a clear identity with a strong set of colours will not only inspire your club but also allow others to aspire to be like your club.

CONSIDER:

- What impression does your club give through its kit and identity?
- Is it easy for players, fans or parents to buy kit?

Other signs that your club is in trouble

There are a few other signs that your club could need help.

A substandard second team or academy

Your club is only as strong as the players within the pipeline. The second team or academy is generally the side that will give you the insight into the health of any club. If the second team is full of ageing first players or out-of-form players, it is often an early sign of cracks within a club. If there is a poor academy, there is no pipeline for any future first team talent.

A second team should be the breeding ground for future first team players. They should be mentored and coached by former first team players. When injuries occur with first team players, then the succession planning is already in place.

A classic error is when a player plays in a particular position or style of play within the second team, and then they get selected for first team but are playing out of position or in a new style of play. This is going to result in creating an out-of-form player. It is imperative that a playing philosophy is created for the entire club.

A disengaged committee

A disengaged committee is the rot that can kill a thriving club. It's like having a ship without a sail or captain; in troubled waters, the ship will go wayward.

The club committee needs to be aligned on a strategic plan and key objectives or targets. If this is done well, the committee will buy into a vision and enjoy meetings. I have spent many years being a disengaged committee member myself and have avoided attending meetings. The key members of a committee need to spend time creating a strategy that is shared with the committee and then the wider membership. With a vision and a plan, most organisations are unstoppable.

An ineffective chair

An overzealous or dormant chair can also ruin a club. A chairperson should try to move on at the point they lose energy or enthusiasm for the club. Most of the time they carry on for years despite not having any interest, their main reason being that there is no natural successor. The members will always have far too much respect for the incumbent chair, and therefore if any members are interested in the role, they won't share their interest until the existing chair has vacated. Only when the existing chair has announced their 'stepping down or retirement' will others declare their interest in the role. An important part of the changing of chairperson is allowing a significant handover period. It's important to make sure any role on a committee is voted on correctly; competition for places is important.

Logos and branding not telling the same story

With poor leadership and direction, the managers and organisers will make decisions by themselves in the interests of their section. Managers may look to adapt the club logo for their section or want to move away from the club colours. What's the net result of this? On the surface, not a lot, but once one area of the club is allowed to not be unified then other areas will join them. Naturally, over time, silos occur. Players will end up being loyal to a team or a section rather than the club as a whole. This then results in poor performance and no pride in the overall organisation.

CASE STUDY: Out of the silos

When **Sean Jarvis** was appointed CEO at **Leicestershire County Cricket Club** (CCC) in 2020, he found out that there were many different sections of the club with different logos. Budgets were kept separate. Even training aids and balls were kept separate. There was a team-first rather than a club-first approach.

Within a few months, he scrapped the multiple logos and made it clear to all sections that they worked, volunteered or played for Leicestershire CCC. The overall impact was that the women's and girls' teams now feel they are part of the club, and their male counterparts partake in their success. First team players are now coaching within women's, girls' and boys' pathways. In 2023 Leicestershire lifted the Royal London Cup ending a twelve-year drought in silverware. There is now a buzz around the club, and all sections are pulling together for Leicestershire CCC, not just their individual section. I'm predicting more silverware in the years to come.

Summary

The problems shared by many clubs are difficulties in recruitment, in creating a talent pipeline and in attracting enough volunteers to help run the club, both on the coaching and administration side. Offering a clear vision for the club can help with this, as can providing motivation in young leadership programmes for juniors and extra rewards for coaches, the Pied Pipers of the club.

If you do not own your pitch or court, you will have to think creatively to ensure a supply of suitable facilities to hire. Think about the impression that you are giving in your online presence (or lack of) and in your kit, logos and branding. The leadership team is responsible for creating the positivity that powers a successful club and this may need a committee overhaul or a new chair.

CONSIDER:

- What is the diagnosis from your health check?
- You probably know what your key problem is, even if you have never voiced it. Are there others you haven't thought of?

3

Why Great Clubs Are Great, And What We Can Learn From Them

Certain clubs have a long track record of success. Your club might look at the competition and feel a level of envy. What is the secret sauce for club glory? It doesn't just occur; years and years of trial and error seem to have created a set of expectations and culture within a successful club.

In this chapter, we'll study New Zealand's All Blacks and Manchester United under Sir Alex Ferguson as supreme examples of a successful environment. Over several years, I've studied these organisations and identified key traits that enable the people within existing or start-up clubs to replicate their levels of success.

How clubs create a successful environment

There are three core groups of people that need to work in harmony to create a successful sports club: the leadership group, coaches, and staff and volunteers. There needs to be a clear set of expectations between the three groups in order for the club to create long-term success on the pitch.

1. The leadership group

This could be in the form of a strong committee, management team, board or ownership. This group of people are the administrators and guardians of the club. They provide leadership alongside strategic and financial direction. Within the Premier League there are many case studies that demonstrate how the leadership of this group of individuals can make an overall impact on a club's performance.

2. Coaches

This group requires support from the leadership team and team managers. Expectations must be laid out by the leadership groups as to what the coaches' goals and targets should be, along with any financial constraints. At grassroots level, a coach's role can be to either create an engagement or performance environment.

An engagement coach creates enjoyment and a love for the sport in order to gain long-term participation from the athletes. The particular focus for this type of coaching is fun, fun, fun. Smiles on players' faces and a willingness to come back week after week will be the key goal. Great engagement coaches become Pied Pipers, often having a group of youngsters that grows exponentially due to word of mouth. It's the leadership groups' responsibility to provide support and resources for the engagement coach.

A performance coach creates an environment in which to win games. Professional coaches create performance environments as they have been tasked to win fixtures, leagues or cups, or to achieve a particular position within a league. Quite often, amateur coaches try to replicate professional coaches' styles but find they ruin the enjoyment for players. It's critical for the leadership team to set expectations for each coach and targets for the season.

3. Staff and volunteers

This group is the backbone of the club's operations. Successful clubs tend to have a base of staff and volunteers which have been involved with the club for a number of years. Professional or semi-professional staff often work partly for love of the organisation as well as for their careers. Volunteers tend to have links to the club, possibly having played for the club themselves or with family that have done so.

Poor leadership groups sometimes overlook the value of this core group and underestimate the length of time spent on tasks behind the scenes. Even within professional clubs, volunteers carry out tasks that poor leadership groups do not know about. If leadership groups do engage with these volunteers, they alone can drive the success of a club.

How the three core groups can work together effectively

Within any organisation – professional or amateur – there are three core principles that underpin a club's success: mission, passion and culture.

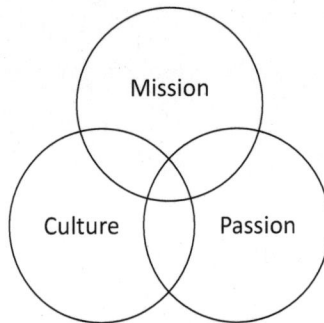

1. Mission

Many clubs do not have a mission statement; they are like a ship without a sail. This type of club will often have conflicts regarding expectations at every level. Should the U15s team be winning or developing?

Should the clubhouse be rented out for commercial use? Without a mission statement, every decision becomes difficult. With no core mission, there are no objectives or focus areas, and therefore no achievement or taste for success.

It's important that leadership teams spend high-quality time working through the strategic direction of the organisation and follow it up with an operational plan for stakeholders to execute. As soon as a plan by the leadership team is vocalised, other stakeholders tend to buy into this plan and results soon follow.

2. Passion

Clubs are fuelled by passion. Passion from the leadership, coaches, staff and volunteers is clearly required. If there is a level of apathy among stakeholders, it's linked to a lack of mission. What is far more common is over-passionate stakeholders who allow their emotions to get in front of rational decision making. Having a mission that's simple and well documented in a visual way often will temper overtly passionate stakeholders within the organisation.

3. Culture = expectation + respect + humility

Respected sporting organisations tend to have a set of expectations. These could be as simple as what to wear to and from a game or saying 'thank you' to the volunteers at the end of each fixture. Without a set of expectations, there tends to be minimal respect for the club; without respect for the club, there tends to be a poor culture. Having a small set of expectations from the leadership and coaching groups is a great way to build a culture of respect. Players that respect every area of the club tend to get respect back.

CONSIDER:

- Does your club have a set of expectations that every player understands?

The winning culture of the All Blacks

It's well documented that over the last century, the most successful sporting organisation is New Zealand's All Blacks. Since their first international test match in 1903, their winning percentage is 76.77%.[1] How has one of the smallest-populated countries in world rugby created a winning culture for such a long period of time?

Rugby as a sport was invented in England and, like most sports, was exported to Commonwealth countries. Rugby was a great fit physically for the Maoris. We could attribute many years of success to the genetic make-up of the indigenous New Zealand team; however, in recent times other countries' physicality matches or beats the All Blacks. How have they continued their winning culture? How can your club learn from this?

Legacy by James Kerr gives us an insight into fifteen core principles that give the All Blacks their culture. Every sports club, no matter how amateur, can replicate these fifteen lessons.

1. Sweep the sheds

Character starts with humility and discipline and it *always* beats talent. The All Blacks have humility at the core of their culture. Regardless of the importance of the fixture, World Cup final or warm-up game, the team will always sweep the changing room after the game. 'Nobody is too big to do the small things.'[2]

2. Go for the gap

Adapt. When you are on top of your game, change your game. Create a culture of always learning plus continuous improvement. The All Blacks are taught to be aware that today's success is going to be tomorrow's failure without commitment to continuous improvement. To be successful, any organisation – be it sporting or business – needs those within to desire personal and professional development.

3. Play with purpose

Play with purpose; the All Blacks play for a higher purpose than themselves. How can you create purpose for your sports club? Is the first team's purpose to inspire juniors?

As Simon Sinek says in *Start With Why*,[3] 'People don't buy what you do, they buy why you do it.' Each club needs to make sure the leadership group, coaches and players all buy into a clear purpose. A clear vision or mission will create the purpose to allow your club to move forward.

4. Take responsibility (pass the ball)

Leaders create leaders. Empower others within the team or club to progress. This creates ownership, accountability and trust within the club.

5. Create a learning environment

People who think they know it all often ruin this step. An always learning culture means the All Blacks alumni become experienced teachers and newly capped players their students.

How can you create a learning environment within your club? The best way is to allow players to fail. Players should not be punished for experimenting, and individuals should be taught the value of learning from their mistakes. You cannot learn without making mistakes. It is how you learn that counts.

6. Don't be a dickhead

No All Black is bigger than their jersey; nobody is bigger than the team. What defines dickhead behaviour is unwritten, but the selfish mindset of individuals will negate the ability to create a collective culture. Senior players must have the courage to let junior players know if they are being dickheads. There is no room for prima donnas. You are either a team player or you are not.

Within grassroots sports, often compromises are made in the culture for a talented player, so coaches and leadership groups allow and accept dickhead behaviour. Once the rot has set in, it will take seasons to change.

7. Have high expectations

Dream big. Aim for the highest cloud. The All Blacks are taught to embrace fear of failure, and cleverly use a healthy loss aversion to motivate even greater performance. Successful organisations have high internal benchmarks; they set their expectations high and try to exceed them.

8. Be prepared

By failing to prepare, you are preparing to fail. Successful organisations train to win. Practice is often far higher in intensity than playing. This creates a mindset to perform and win. Successful organisations such as the US Navy Seals replicate the All Blacks' theory of practice under pressure. As James Kerr says in *Legacy*, 'Most people have the will to win; few have the will to prepare to win'.[4]

9. Think clearly under pressure

Don't lose your head; no hotheads allowed. The ability to think clearly under pressure is a life skill. Decision making under pressure can separate the best teams from the worst. Calm heads think clearly and accurately under pressure; hotheads tend to miss opportunities.

The leadership coaches need to not only create pressure cooker environments in training to allow players to train, fail and reflect, they also need to manage parents, who can often be a trigger for hotheaded players.

10. Be authentic

Keep it real. Know thyself. Self-awareness is the most important part of a healthy team culture. If you understand how you come across, you can learn to adapt yourself. High-performance teams can eyeball each other and give honest feedback without hotheaded behaviour.

11. Invent your own language

The All Blacks have rituals, songs and stories that bind them together to create a culture that is passed down from generation to generation. It's a common language that everyone understands within the All Blacks team.

CONSIDER:

- Does your club have customs?
- Does it have stories to share, a club song or maybe a ritual before or after each game?

12. Make sacrifices

Champions sacrifice. The All Blacks constantly ask themselves whether they could do more.

Champions do extra. It could be as simple as being the first to turn up to and the last to leave training sessions. Good is not good enough. High standards breed high standards.

13. Create rituals to create a culture

Inspiring leaders create rituals that bind their team together. For the All Blacks, the team culture is based on over a century of heritage. What could you do to create a culture for your club?

14. Be a good ancestor

Plant trees that you will never see. The All Blacks connect the past, present and future. They often talk about leaving the jersey in a better place than when they first wore it. They obsess over those that wore their number before them. Understand that there were giants that came before you and you are standing on their shoulders.

15. Write your legacy

'This is your time.'[5] The All Blacks understand that this is their time. They wear the black jersey with purpose and pride and receive a small book featuring shirts from the legendary teams of the past. Each book has blank pages for the player to fill in. It's a hugely powerful message that impresses upon the new player, no matter what has gone before, you have the ability to create your own history.

CONSIDER:

- How can you apply this principle to your club?
- Is it an honours board? A set of awards?
- How can you allow players to build their own legacy?

The Sir Alex Ferguson formula

As a North London boy and an Arsenal fan, it hurts me to say this: Sir Alex Ferguson is arguably the best coach of all time. Sorry Mr Wenger. Sir Alex spent twenty-six seasons at Manchester United, winning thirteen league titles and twenty-six other domestic and international trophies. That's almost twice as many as any other coach.

If you are a coach or part of a club's leadership team, let's explore how we can take some lessons from Sir Alex and inspire some ideas for your own club. In Sir Alex's final year at Manchester United, he spent time with Harvard Business School professor Anita Elberse. She studied him and talked to those that worked with him to identified a number of unique traits that created Sir Alex's philosophy.

1. Start with the foundation

From the moment he joined Manchester United, Sir Alex invested, time, effort and resources on the youth of the organisation. He created centres of excellence, nurturing a pipeline of talent. He recognised young players could be moulded and be part of a club-wide playing philosophy, which would be translated into playing the 'Manchester United way'.

Sir Alex recognised that in order to achieve long-term success, he needed to build a club, not just a good first team: 'I wanted to build right from the bottom. That was to create fluency and a continuity of supply to the first team.'[6] In this way, Sir Alex argued, the players would all grow up together and the resulting bond would naturally create a team spirit.

CONSIDER:

- Does your club have a strong pipeline of youth talent?

---

2. Dare to rebuild your team

Regardless of how many trophies or league titles the current team might have won, Sir Alex was never scared of rebuilding his team. In his twenty-six seasons, he built five winning squads. It's difficult to maintain a winning side unless there are constant improvements. As Manchester United legend Ryan Giggs said, 'He's never really looking at this moment, he's always looking into the future.'[7]

Sir Alex's strategy took advantage of longevity – he expected to stay in his position and could afford to plan for the future. He explained, 'I believe that the cycle of a successful team lasts maybe four years, and then some change is needed. We tried to visualise the team three or four years ahead and make decisions accordingly.'[8]

He identified three levels of players: those thirty and older, those aged roughly twenty-three to thirty, and younger players coming in. The idea was that the younger players were developing and would meet the standards that the older ones had set.

3. Set high standards – and hold everyone to them

Sir Alex was passionate about instilling values in his players. His team building, team preparation, motivational talks and tactical decisions all served to maintain the standards Manchester United had set as a football club. He never allowed a bad training session, believing that 'What you see in training manifests itself on the game field.' He insisted on a focus on quality, so players would improve with each session, 'It was about intensity, concentration, speed – a high level of performance.'[9]

CONSIDER:

- What are the standards at your club?
- How do you create a culture to hold everyone accountable?

4. Never, ever cede control

The coaches and leadership team need to be led. Sir Alex made sure his authority was known throughout the club: 'If the players decided how the training should be, what days they should have off, what the discipline should be, and what the tactics should be – then Manchester United would not be the Manchester United we know.'[10]

5. Match the message to the moment

Sir Alex was always on the sidelines, shouting and screaming at players and officials. However, this was how he behaved for ninety minutes per match, not for the rest of his week. He was known to adapt his style and vary his approach to suit his team and individuals. Every individual might need a different approach. He described how, 'As a manager, you play different roles at different times. Sometimes you have to be a doctor, or a teacher, or a father.'[11]

6. Prepare to win

Sir Alex implemented a similar philosophy to the All Blacks with regards to training. 'We practice for when the going gets tough, so we know what it takes to be successful in those situations,' one of United's assistant coaches told *Harvard Business Review*.[12]

Training with purpose and pressure resulted in Manchester United's ability to win games in the second half and final minutes. United had a better record when tied at half-time or with 15 minutes left to play than any other club in the English league. Sir Alex reflected, 'I think all my teams had perseverance – they never gave in […] it is amazing to see what can happen in the dying seconds of a match.'[13]

7. Rely on the power of observation

Coaches and leadership teams in any organisation need to have strong observational skills. Sir Alex explained, 'The ability to see things is key – or, more specifically, the ability to see things you don't expect to see.'[14]

He noted that the switch from coaching to observing allowed him to better evaluate his players and their performances: 'As a coach on the field, you don't see everything. A regular observer, however, can spot changes in training patterns, energy levels, and work rates.'[15]

8. Never stop adapting

During Sir Alex's reign the world of football changed, as did the wider world. Everything from the finances within the game through to sports science evolved. David Gill, former CEO of Manchester United, said Ferguson 'demonstrated a tremendous capacity to adapt as the game has changed.'[16]

On-pitch, Sir Alex fielded a team predominately made up of youngsters. He was heavily criticised for it, but today we see it as common practice within the Premier League.

Off the field, he put emphasis on creating a large back-room staff. He appointed a team of sports scientists to support the coaches. Following their suggestions, he installed Vitamin D booths in the players' dressing room in order to compensate for the lack of sunlight in Manchester, and championed the use of vests fitted with GPS sensors that allow an analysis of performance just 20 minutes after a training session. He was the first coach to employ an optometrist for his players. United also hired a yoga instructor to work with players twice a week and in 2014 unveiled a state-of-the-art medical facility at its training ground so that all procedures short of surgery could be handled on-site. This ensured a level of discretion impossible in a public hospital, where details about a player's condition are invariably leaked to the press.

Clearly, this level of resource is only available to the wealthiest clubs in the world, so how can we learn from Sir Alex's philosophy of 'never stop adapting'?

CONSIDER:

- Could it be as simple as utilising social media to communicate to the members?
- Could it be increasing female participation within your club to make it more diverse and inclusive?
- Could it be utilising an app for match availability?

Summary

It's important to learn from the elite level and transfer the learnings to your grassroots club. Learning from the All Blacks and Manchester United, we can clearly see that when the leadership group and coaches are aligned on ambition, responsibility, culture and targets, it will trickle down to players. When the players are clearer on the expectations of the club, they will ultimately perform better.

In the next section we will investigate my C+L+U=B framework to unpack how we create the conditions for success.

CONSIDER:

- Do you have a pipeline of talent within your club?
- Are ambitions aligned within your club stakeholders?
- Is there clarity on responsibilities, culture and targets?

PART TWO
THE C+L+U=B FRAMEWORK

I've been fortunate enough to work with thousands of clubs around the world, from grassroots level through to the top tier of international sport, and the common thread throughout every sports club or organisation is the passion given by the people who run them.

Whether a single or multi-sports club, grassroots or professional, I have noticed a number of traits that result in the creation of a successful sports club. When a club moves away from these traits is when the club loses its identity and membership.

In this section, we'll unpack the C+L+U=B framework.

C.L.U.B.

Community +

Every club is a vital part of its community. Community brings people of all backgrounds together with commonality. Without a strong community there is no C.L.U.B.

Leadership +

Clubs play a vital part in growing leaders. Not only on the pitch but in everyday life. We believe the club representatives and the volunteer coaches should be leaders who inspire the next generation of leaders.

Unify =

In a selfie world of individualism, team sports have the power to shed personal identity and enable individuals to be a part of something bigger than themselves.

A single identity through kit unifies the club as one.

Belong

A good club creates a sense of belonging for individuals. This not only means the players on the pitch but also the volunteers that make the club run. Every person has a vital part to play in the C.L.U.B. ecosystem.

What's our C+L+U=B philosophy?

4
Community

Team sports have the power to unite people from all backgrounds. They provide a common goal – irrelevant of wealth, age, race, gender or sexuality. All kinds of people love to watch, support and play team sports. They also need an opposition, be it in a friendly kickabout or when playing tennis-ball cricket in the street.

At the professional end of the sporting pyramid, clubs have a core fanbase that are likely to be located within the local community. From a grassroots perspective, the club has a role to play as a place for health and fitness and social gatherings. Sports clubs provide a physical focal point within the community for playing competitively, training or just having a bit of unstructured fun with friends.

To the players and members, the physical focal point is also an emotional connection to the place they call home. The benefits of grassroots sports clubs to the local community outside of the on-field elements include the ability to socialise at these venues. I've had countless parties and events throughout my life at my local cricket club. In some places, the local community doesn't have options for a social life outside of these sports clubs.

Rugby clubs are at the heart of the community in Wales, cricket clubs in Lancashire and Yorkshire, and grassroots football clubs in Northern Ireland. The club in many of these locations is the focal point of the community. Club rivalries stem back generations, and the clubs can generate a huge level of interest, attendance and revenue when local derbies take place.

The power of sporting community is symbolised by the Christmas truce in World War I. On Christmas Eve 1914, both German and British soldiers were in trenches close to each other on the Western Front. They could hear each other singing carols, and messages were shouted between trenches. Christmas Day dawned and the rival soldiers met in no man's land. They exchanged gifts, took photos and, most importantly, played a game of football against each other. Boxing Day arrived and the sides went back to war. This story is one of the best examples of the power of sport breaking through community, regardless of the wider context of World War I.

Community as social capital

If you are part of the leadership of a sports club, it's imperative to make sure you think of the bigger picture alongside the running of the club. You should be aware of the term 'social capital' (or 'social value'). The definition of social capital is: 'The networks of relationships among people who live and work in a particular society, enabling that society to function effectively.'[17] Social capital is an economic theory that recognises the direct link of all stakeholders within an organisation trusting each other. This stems from high-quality communication that takes place within all levels of an organisation. A sports club has good social capital when all stakeholders within the club are connected to it.

For sports clubs, I like to replace the phrase 'social capital' with 'community'. Sports clubs – in particular, grassroots sports clubs – are a vital part of the social ecosystem that is not valued. Clubs need to make sure they never forget their vital role within a community.

Sports clubs have obvious physical and mental health benefits to society. This is not unique to a single country or continent. The benefits sports clubs bring are the same globally. Their wider impact on the community is quite often intangible. Social, cultural, economic and urban development impacts are intangible positive factors that sports clubs can give to their local

61

community. Make sure you are aware of all these areas when making decisions about your club.

Every successful club is at the heart of its community, and the people that run the club need to have the community in their minds, front and centre. These clubs need to be inclusive and accessible to all, and the leadership within them should be happy to support community groups, events and indeed businesses, if required.

The benefits of community engagement

The English Football League (EFL) is three leagues below the Premier League. It currently consists of seventy-two member clubs. The EFL published a report in January 2023 entitled 'Measuring the impact of EFL clubs in the community',[18] in which data was gathered from EFL clubs between 2019 and 2022 and analysed. The report concluded that the EFL clubs and their community outreach programmes have generated a social value of £865m.

The seventy-two EFL member clubs have some groundbreaking statistics which other sports should try to replicate:

- £101m in funding raised and investment
- 6,744 partnerships developed

- 9,922 staff, coaches and volunteers deployed into the community

- £40.8m in facility and other in-kind support

- 840,000 participants engaged in 2021–22

If you are a grassroots club, you may already be engaging within your community. By keeping track of the numbers, you will not only be able to improve but you will also need this data to apply for funds from your local authority and other grant-making organisations.

A club that takes the time to engage and widen its net throughout its local community will always get a huge level of rewards back. By taking a little time to understand the local community, your committee will identify and recruit new members and volunteers. You will attract people who will support club projects that the club might need more hands to complete – everything from coaching through to fixing up the clubhouse. By actively engaging, you will also be able to attract more funding for grants. Funders are increasingly looking to support inclusive organisations that have a good track record of community engagement.

Here are some of the benefits of engaging the wider community:

- Promoting education, even something as simple as better-spoken English from migrant communities.

- Reducing anti-social behaviour in the local area by getting youngsters off the streets to play sports instead.

- Creating a sense of pride in the area. When people are involved in projects to do with their community, they gain a sense of pride and belonging.

At the start of the Covid-19 pandemic, sports clubs were not allowed to play. When sports were back on, clubs were not allowed to have fans in attendance. This resulted in a huge financial impact for these clubs that relied on the sale of tickets to fans attending fixtures. There were, however, some magical stories of sports clubs supporting their local community in those dark times:

- Tranmere Rovers supported over 1,000 vulnerable people from the local community in tackling loneliness.[19]

- Darlington FC designed and implemented a buddy scheme for fans that were vulnerable.[20]

- Stevenage FC supported locals who needed medicine delivered by creating a community care line.[21]

- Stockport County FC donated £75,000 for the Stockport NHS Foundation Trust Charitable Fund to help treatment towards coronavirus within the local community.[22]

- Many Premier League players and managers phoned fans to make sure they had medical supplies and food if they needed.[23]

CASE STUDY: A warm sporting welcome for young migrants

Beeston Hockey Club is one of the largest hockey clubs in the East Midlands, with about 800 members. The club has a long history of developing national talent and playing in the top leagues in England.

Based in Nottingham, the club were approached by local charity **Belong**, which supports migrant families settling into the Nottingham community. First team players supported the partnership by delivering twelve weeks of training sessions for young migrants who had located to Nottingham. The new club members have felt engaged and welcome, with hockey as their commonality. Most of the new players didn't speak English, but improved their English significantly during the twelve weeks.

The club also launched a school uniform programme. Club members could donate either new or good-condition used school uniform to the migrant families to help them out financially.

These small gestures have embraced the new families that they have supported as part of the community, who will never forget their welcome to Nottingham by Beeston Hockey Club.

How can we connect with local community groups?

The first step is to create a checklist of all the different areas within your community that you might be able to reach out to:

- Women and girls

- Disabled people

- Older people

- LGBTQIA+

- People of ethnic diversity

- People of religious diversity, eg Jews, Hindus, Muslims

- Lower social-economic groups

CASE STUDY: They couldn't wait for diversity

During the 1960s and 1970s, a large group of Asian migrants left East Africa and moved to the UK. Many families settled in Leicester as their skills led them to work in the clothing industry that was based there.

The **Guru Nanak Football Club** (GNG FC) was formed in Leicester in 1969 by young Asian men who were not being selected or welcomed in other local clubs within the city. The predominantly Sikh players formed the club with the help of their local Gurdwara. With passion and drive, they ended up owning their own centre and grounds. At the time, the GNG FC was the only black, Asian and minority ethnic (BAME) club in the UK. Now over fifty years old, the club is thriving and going from strength to strength with a strong girls' section.

This club is particularly close to my heart as the pain the founders felt would have been the same pain felt by my uncles and father when they made the journey from East Africa to North London and tried to join sports clubs there.

Today, we see migrants from Ukraine and Syria. Will they be in a similar situation to the founders of GNG, not feeling welcome in sports clubs due to the lack of cultural integration, or can we now do better?

Society has changed significantly over the last few decades. It was only in 1971 that the FA lifted a fifty-year ban on women playing football. It's no surprise that pockets of society were not welcomed into sports clubs, which tended to favour the white, heterosexual, able-bodied male. Many good players of different backgrounds within the local community were overlooked, not selected or simply not welcomed, so what did they do? They created their own community clubs.

CASE STUDY: Opening football up to the girls

A diverse membership of your club can only do good, yet 50% of the population – women and girls – have in many cases been explicitly told that team sports are not for them.

Passionate about football, **Fleur Cousens** heard this all her life. In 2015, she launched **Goal Diggers FC**, based in London, and set about creating the most inclusive and accessible football club for women and non-binary people.

Fleur created a strong team of leaders who bought into her philosophy of inclusivity, and the club grew quickly. Membership prices were kept as low as possible, and selection was all about availability rather than ability. Fleur's day job is in TV production, which is obvious when you take a look at the club website.

When I met Fleur in 2021, I thought Goal Diggers FC was one of the most creative clubs I'd come across. When I first spoke to her, she explained that the club's biggest problem was access to pitches. The press the club received, within London and nationally, brought on an unexpected level of demand. She was frustrated that more established but smaller clubs were getting the premium timeslots on pitches. The last time I spoke to her, she told me the club was up to 240 players, with a waiting list of fifty plus.

Goal Diggers welcomes players of all ages, races and sexuality. Winning and ability is not the focus, fun and inclusivity is. Fleur worked out that there was a large community that was not catered for and created a club that catered for their needs.

Those 240-plus women could have joined your female section, but maybe they didn't feel catered for?

CONSIDER:

- What is stopping your club from opening its doors to an underrepresented group?
- What would be the benefits of doing this?

Fan assisted: the Portsmouth FC story

Fans are the backbone of a professional club's community. They can make or break a club, even rescue it in its hour of need. Portsmouth FC is a prime example of this.

I was fortunate to start working with Portsmouth FC in 2007, while working for another kit supplier, Canterbury of New Zealand. When the club was bought by Alexandre Gaydamak, a new era was born and fresh financial power was given to the leadership team.

I was quite young in my career and had never been to Portsmouth before. I would often stay in a hotel and I remember going for a walk around Portsmouth and noticing the football club's moon and stars logo on road signs. The club was literally stamped onto every street corner – there was no getting away from it. It turned out that the club's logo was shared by the local council and almost every major institute in the city. The club's nickname, 'Pompey', was also the city's nickname. Local businesses were named after it: Pompey Garage, Pompey Fish and Chip Shop.

The club was everywhere, deeply built into the psyche of the city of Portsmouth.

Harry Redknapp, who joined Portsmouth for a second time, built a dream squad made up of some of the best players of the time. In May 2008, with this well-built squad, Portsmouth went on to lift the FA Cup. The city was raving. They hadn't seen this triumph since 1939.

I was part of the team that moved the club kit away from its signature royal blue shirt, white shorts and red socks to an all-royal-blue kit. The fans revolted for a short period. This was my first taste of the importance of kit as an identity for a club, and my first taste of passionate fans. Social media was in its early days, so fans only had a few places they could voice their opinions – I think if we did it today, there would be a serious amount of backlash on social media. It was all forgotten as Pompey lifted the cup.

A year later, the club was sold again and the wheels started to fall off. The club went into administration, not just once but twice. I had moved on but as Pompey had been the first Premier League club I had worked with, I kept a close eye on their progress.

In 2013, The Portsmouth Supporters Trust (PST) bought their beloved football club from the administrators and it became the largest community-owned football club in England. The PST raised about £2m via a share-ownership scheme. The individuals and fans bought each community share at a price of £1,000.

If you wanted to become a president, the investment was £50,000. Those investing £100,000 or more would sit on an advisory board. The club also created a Pompey lottery scheme to raise funds, £2 per ticket per week. Over 2,000 Portsmouth fans invested in this well-thought-through set of options to raise funds to save the club. Other funds came from the City Council and a private property developer who was interested in purchasing the surrounding land the club owned.

The administrators were sceptical about the prospects of a community-based scheme being successful, as no club the size of Portsmouth with a debt of £17.4m had been rescued in this way before. Portsmouth was different: the city's flagship export was in trouble and its community came to the rescue.

This story has a Disney ending. In 2017, under the instruction of the fans, the PST sold their shares to The Tornante Company, an investment company owned by former Disney CEO, Michael Eisner. He confirmed a long-term approach to the club and further investment. He still owns the club in 2024 (at the time of writing) and work has now started to increase the capacity at Fratton Park stadium.

Summary

Community is integral to the success of a club – not just the community created within the club of players, volunteers and staff but also the surrounding community. It's worth measuring your club's community engagement, as what is measured can be improved. Think about how you can extend your community engagement by reaching out to under-represented groups. In professional clubs, the fanbase can make or break the club.

For grassroots community, belonging is created first within the club, which then attracts family, friends and others who will support and volunteer for the club.

CONSIDER:

- Does your club have a strong sense of community?
- What sort of community does your club strive for?
- What can your club do to encourage more players, volunteers and fans to become part of its community?
- How would your club benefit from having a stronger community?

5
Leadership

The inherent nature of sports clubs means we focus on pitch or court success and leadership. It's often said, the best teams don't just have a captain and a coach but every player has a leadership role. In elite high-performance sport, under-pressure leadership on the pitch is put to the test.

Grassroots clubs also play a vital part in growing leaders. Clubs have the unique ability to give leadership opportunities to young people – the obvious being captaincy. Clearly, a captain must have respect and trust from their teammates to make the right decisions under pressure during games.

Not every player within the club will be successful on the pitch. How else can we develop leaders? How can we identify the leaders of the future?

The leadership team: how many people do you need?

Every sports club – grassroots or professional – is led by people. The success of the club will be determined by how this leadership team leads and delivers the club's annual programme.

This leadership team, group or committee should be voted for by the membership on an annual basis (unless it's a professional or privately owned organisation). It should be obsessive about every step towards achieving the goals agreed, which could be as simple as setting up and packing away equipment, collecting subscription fees, coaching the players or recruiting sponsors. Every member of this committee or leadership group should bring a positive impact to the club and the wider community.

When planning the annual programme for the club, or a particular event, it is important to identify how many people are needed to lead. Once you have identified this number, figure out what skills they need to make the programme or event a success.

When recruiting any leadership team, it's important to recognise the diversity of those you are serving within the club. The more diverse your leadership team, the more likely you are to be successful in representing your community.

CONSIDER:

- Does your club need more women?
- Does your club have representation from a minority group or religious background?
- Does your club truly understand disability requirements?

What does a committee look like?

A committee is the group of people that lead the governance of a club. Initially, they might not be voted on as the club starts out; however, as the club grows it's important to have an annual general meeting and allow club members to vote for committee members.

Even for a simple club committee, as a minimum you need a chair, treasurer, secretary and at least one coach or team captain. The specific leadership roles may vary depending on the size, structure and nature of the sports club. I've broken down the roles and outlined the skills needed for each one in Chapter 12.

Try to keep the committee to between seven and ten people. The larger the committee, the less agile your club becomes.

Recruiting good leaders

You need some leaders. What tactics can you use to attract them? Try the following:

- **Word of mouth:** Think about the network the club already has. Who within the club or one step away from it – perhaps a parent or grandparent of a player – could join or support the leadership team?

- **Create recruitment materials:** Get some flyers or posters that can be placed within the local community (in supermarkets, places of worship and community centres). You will be surprised at how many people with the time and the right skills might want to get involved.

- **Open days:** Open days for the local community are a great way of recruiting leadership talent.

Common traits of good leaders

Good leaders are willing to take on the responsibilities and challenges of a variety of situations or people. Whether that be at your club or in your workplace, good leaders have common traits that can be identified:

- **They motivate others and set an example:** Be it at seven or seventy years old, good leaders will motivate others. They find the positives and create excitement in the most mundane tasks. They also are quick to establish trust and encourage other members. A positive aura will mean others in the club will follow, which creates retention of members and, in turn, loyalty to the club.

- **They are humble and self-aware:** Good leaders are approachable as they have a level of humility. The majority of leaders have a high level of self-awareness. They know how they can be perceived and what they need to do to adapt their style. This means they can rouse a changing room, galvanise a team or recruit volunteers.

- **They are always learning:** Good leaders understand that to improve they need to learn. They are happy to learn from others and are always looking to develop their skills.

- **They look forward and express passion:** Good leaders will not only manage what they have in the present but they will also provide clarity for the future of the organisation. Any sports club is going to be filled with passionate people, but some members will only be passionate about winning. Victories will be balanced with losses – that's the beauty of sport – and leaders need to be able to lead throughout good times and bad.

- **They communicate and motivate well:** Good leaders will communicate well and regularly to all in their team. They will have a finger on the pulse of the team. There are all kinds of tasks within a club that really do need motivated volunteers, such as cleaning the clubhouse at the beginning of the season or running the bar on a club night. Good leaders will motivate others to take on these volunteer tasks.

- **They make decisions:** Leaders are always looked upon to make difficult decisions, sometimes under pressure.

- **They are great listeners:** Good leaders will take the time to listen to and understand opinions and take on board any feedback to improve.

- **They are flexible:** Good leaders can adapt their style to different people or situations. They can use various styles or strategies to work with different people.

- **They reduce conflict:** Leaders will nip problems in the bud. Reducing conflict and maintaining relationships throughout the club is a natural skill of leaders.

- **They find solutions:** Leaders will identify ways of improving the club. All clubs have problems; it's the people that come up with the solutions that are the true leaders.

What are the different styles of leadership?

In any sporting organisation, you will come across many different personality profiles and leadership styles. It's important to recognise and embrace all of them.

Autocratic leadership

The autocratic leadership style is not very self-aware and does not take others into consideration when making decisions. This style of leader makes the decisions and dictates what is being done, believing that leading from the front is the best method. Sir Alex Ferguson is the best example of an autocratic leader.

Democratic leadership

The democratic leader asks others for input before making decisions. This makes the team feel as though their voices are heard and their opinions are valued. One of the best examples of a democratic leadership style can be seen in the Premier League, with Jürgen Klopp while he was at Liverpool FC. He has shown on many occasions that he has a democratic leadership style by engaging his players and gaining feedback. He makes the players feel valued by allowing their input. This increases players' motivation and improves results.

Laissez-faire leadership

This style of leadership is a leader who leads from the back of the room and doesn't want the limelight: almost the opposite of autocratic leadership. Laissez-faire leaders will often know the direction or decision that needs to happen, but they will allow others to debate and form a decision. Within coaching, this means an athlete-led approach with minimal guidance from the coach. This style lends itself to allowing the team to make mistakes and poor decisions. It's highly likely that in the short term it will lead to poor performance and results.

What is the most effective leadership style?

Lewin, Lippet & White (1939)[24] decided that the most effective form of leadership was the democratic leadership style. Too much autocratic leadership can lead to athletes and players deciding that they no longer wish to work with a coach and refusing to follow instructions, whereas a laissez-faire leader can potentially lead to teams becoming disorganised and not performing well.

When Jürgen Klopp was appointed Liverpool FC manager in 2015, he was coming off the back of almost two decades of Manchester United and Chelsea dominance. Liverpool was one of the largest clubs in Europe, but it lacked leadership. Matthew Smith, senior lecturer in sport and exercise psychology in the Department of Sport, Exercise and Health at the University of Winchester, and Sean Figgins, senior lecturer in sport and exercise psychology and research methods at the University of Chichester, identified five ways he helped change Liverpool's fortunes.[25] All five are relevant to your club:

1. Leaders should create a clear vision

The leadership group creates a vision that all stakeholders buy into. Initially, this needs the coaches to be the first set of stakeholders, outside of the committee, who buy into the created vision.

Klopp was transparent about his playing philosophy. He stated on a number of occasions, 'I believe in a playing philosophy that is emotional, very fast and very strong.' He added, 'It is important to have a playing philosophy that reflects your own mentality, reflects the club and gives you a clear direction to follow.'

Klopp, with the help of the leadership team, started to train existing players and recruit new players that fit this playing philosophy and vision.

2. Leaders need to represent their club's identity

In 2023, eight years into his role at Liverpool, Klopp was still standing by his vision of the club. He was emotional on the sidelines, during interviews his passion was obvious and he made high demands of his players. On several occasions, his celebrations and post-match interviews have caused controversy. He doesn't hide his own emotions, which has sometimes got him into trouble with referees, the Premier League, the FA and the media.

CONSIDER:

- How can you make the best use of passionate individuals in your club?

3. Leaders must reinforce belief and create trust

Klopp is personally intertwined with his playing philosophy. He joined Liverpool from Borussia Dortmund and brought with him their style of play and philosophy. His reputation gave clarity to all stakeholders, in particular, players. By Klopp being so headstrong in his commitment to his vision, he inspired belief from his young players and created a high level of trust with them.

Repeating the same things to players and stakeholders means that eventually they will believe and therefore trust in them. Stable decision making and gaining the trust of players is absolutely the key to inspiring players.

Former Liverpool player Sadio Mané said, 'He is a great person. I trust him blindly, like most of the dressing room.'

4. Leaders need to develop strong connections with players

If you watch Klopp and his staff before and after matches, you will have noticed their physicality with the players. Before a game, Klopp would be on the pitch for the warm-up, high-fiving players and patting them on the back. Post-game, if the players had done well, they would receive hugs from Klopp. He is also known to really understand what is going on with each of his players.

CONSIDER:

- How do your coaches and other leaders show their connection with the players?

5. Leaders should create and deliver goals

When Klopp arrived at Liverpool in October 2015, he stated he would win the Premier League within four years (forty-eight months). He lifted the trophy fifty-six months later. (I'm sure the fans wouldn't hold a grudge against him for his maths.) That is the goal he externally set for all stakeholders to focus on, alongside himself.

Within that same target period, the club also won the following trophies:

1. UEFA Champions League (2018/19)

2. UEFA Super Cup (2019)

3. FIFA Club World Cup (2019)

Winning such high-profile trophies allowed Klopp to reinforce points one to four above and also focus the entire club on the Big Hairy Ambitious Goals (BHAG) of the Premier League.

For grassroots clubs, the BHAG don't need to be about trophies. They could be about recruitment of players, the number of girls playing or anything the leadership group might want to focus on. Set targets and goals that are scary. You will be surprised how much it focuses your club to achieve them.

CONSIDER:

- What is your BHAG? Choose something that might seem a long way off to you now.

Create leadership opportunities for all

You have identified a number of people who have strong leadership skills. They could be teenagers, retired people or mums that used to play. How do you get them involved?

Induction

Do you take new volunteers through a club induction process? If not, here are a few things to consider. It's worthwhile formalising this process as it means that all your volunteers are given all the information they need from the beginning.

Here is a brief checklist of what to include in your induction for all future leaders:

- Club development plan
- Club history
- Current club size, team training dates, etc
- Introduction to committee members
- Tour of facilities, eg the clubhouse
- Club policies and procedures
- Code of conduct
- Health and safety information
- Insurance
- Safeguarding and DBS
- Their role as a leader
- Understanding what the club needs from them
- Understanding what they want from their experience
- Their main point of contact

Role

It's important to give a top line job specification for volunteers and potential future leaders. Having a good understanding that is documented means that there is clarity for the volunteer. Indicate where the volunteer will have autonomy and where the checkpoints will be. Including some room for autonomy makes it more likely that the volunteer will take ownership of the role.

CASE STUDY: Giving leadership opportunities to young people

Hatch Warren Tigers Netball Club in Basingstoke was launched during the pandemic. Their chair, **Carla Paterson**, is a passionate sports enthusiast as a player, coach and school PE teacher. She set up the Tigers because the nearest club was an hour's drive away. We met on X (formerly Twitter) and I supported her through the process of setting up the committee and operating the club. She launched in April 2021 and six months later had over 200 girls playing netball and a waiting list.

In early 2022, she phoned me with an interesting problem. She said she wanted to get a monthly magazine created but the committee members were too stretched. I had a simple response: have you asked your club members? Have you spoken to the girls? She hadn't considered asking the teenage membership as an option.

Within a few weeks, a magazine was launched. At their first end-of-season event, I was asked to present

---

awards. I met the fourteen-year-old who was the magazine editor. She told me she wasn't very good at netball, but relished the opportunity to create the club's magazine. She told me she worked on it in between her studies and now she wants to go into journalism. I was blown away: here a leadership opportunity within the club had been grasped by a fourteen-year-old. Her parents were so proud of her.

Carla created a new leader by simply asking the membership.

Summary

In this chapter we have identified the characteristics of good leaders and looked at how you can grow your own. We have also looked at leadership styles and suggested that you follow Jürgen Klopp's path at Liverpool FC's in creating and representing a clear vision and identity, reinforcing belief and creating trust, building strong connections with players and creating BHAGs. We have also learnt how Carla Paterson at Hatch Warren Tigers created leadership opportunities within a grassroots club.

CONSIDER:

- Who are the potential leaders in your club now?
- Are there any roles that can be created?
- Have you looked at all areas of the membership to recruit for this role?

6
Unify

As CEO of KitKing, I am passionate about sports kit and its role in achieving excellence on and off the pitch. It is something that came from playing sport at Loughborough University. In 2001, I was a fresher at the UK's top sports university. I chose Loughborough because I wanted to play cricket and be part of a campus university.

Coming from a state grammar school with a traditional approach to uniform, I was surprised to find that there was no unified approach to sports kit, even though more than fifty sports were being played at a high level. There were fifty-plus different brands, designs and colour palettes. Some clubs played in maroon, others in purple; some clubs played in black, others in navy. It was a mess. The university had no interest in a unified approach. Each club had its own identity rather than a single identity for the university.

By 2004, I had been voted on to various committees. I was vice-chair of cricket, treasurer of my hall and chair of the social secretaries. I ran for vice-president of the students union on the manifesto of a unified kit deal. I was elected, had many meetings with the vice chancellor and within twenty-four months of my appointment, the university and all fifty-plus sports clubs agreed on a unified approach. They would all play for Loughborough Students, which would be written beneath the university logo on all kit, all of which would be purple.

The university went out to tender. A number of brands submitted tender and eventually a partner brand was appointed; this partnership is still in place in 2023. This set my vision of the importance of kit.

Why does matching kit matter?

Sports kits or uniforms have a functional role on the pitch or court to enable teams to identify each other, but the unique nature of each kit runs deeper than a functional on-field need.

In nature, members of the same species look alike and this allows strong visual recognition. We now live in a diverse world with society becoming integrated, therefore identity is no longer about race, creed or colour. We are becoming less tribal as a species; however, we still yearn to be part of something. Identifying ourselves as a group or tribe is part of human nature.

For over 5,000 years, there is evidence that humans have tried to create a form of unification that identifies individuals with a wider tribe. It is common for gangs to have their own methods of unification through clothing, graffiti, hand signs, colours and tattoos. As far back as the ice age, humans used tattoos to identify tribes, ownership, social status and also familial ties, symbols and philosophies.

In the 1600s, the first criminal street gangs were recorded in London, when more than twenty gangs were on the loose within the city. They all had a common identifier: a coloured ribbon attached to their clothes. Gangs may also wear colours to identify themselves; for example, the criminal street gangs in LA are the Bloods, who wear red and the Crips, who wear blue.

The functional and emotional roles of kit

Having a strong identity and a unique set of colours is paramount to the success of a club. Kit and identity play a hugely emotional role in club life, from the precision of the club's colours through to the product selection and fit. The cost of the kit is also a huge factor.

If you volunteer to manage the kit, make sure you engage with your membership. Identify the key stakeholders and ask their opinions. I would recommend an online survey or poll to guide you in the right direction of price, quality, colours and product selection. Make sure you are transparent with your membership and give results back to the wider club. By taking the membership on a journey regarding kit and unification, you will gain trust from them to make the right decision.

CASE STUDY: What the Arsenal sleeves say

Arsenal is one of the longest established clubs in England, founded in 1886 by a group of workers from the Woolwich Arsenal Armament Factory. Originally, their kit was inspired by a number of the players who used to play for Nottingham Forest. A few spare kits were gifted and deep red was duly the club's anointed colour. The unique white collar and sleeves were introduced by Herbert Chapman in about 1925, and are still worn today.

It's not quite known when it was introduced, but Arsenal has another unique tradition that unifies their team one step further than their playing shirt colour. The captain would choose for the entire team the length of sleeve shirt they would be playing in; they would wear either long or short sleeves and the entire team would follow suit.

It is a tradition of respect for the captain and a unification that existed until about 2016 when a few players broke the tradition, starting with Theo Walcott.

It's no coincidence that performances dipped when the club lost a few traditions around this time.

Mikel Arteta was a player under Arsène Wenger and appointed club manager in 2019. He was cajoled by supporters to reinstate the lost traditions, in particular the sleeve tradition.

Unifying your club

Having your sports club unified with the same brand, colours and logos will make it look like a professional outfit. This in turn will make players feel like they belong to a pro club, which will increase their confidence. The positive energy that an increase in players' confidence brings is amazing; it will create an increase in win rate on the pitch. When you win more games, you attract better players and coaches. When a club's membership increases, you attract more fans, members and volunteers. By having this additional headcount around the club, the club becomes more well organised overall.

Why does unifying your club matter?

The highest-performing clubs require players to travel, train and obviously play in unified kit. Grassroots clubs are unlikely to be able to achieve that level of detail. However, you can start by making sure that your kit on the pitch is 100% unified. I've worked with many football teams whereby the 'home and training' kit is unified, but the away kits are the manager's choice. This results in divisions when the team uses this kit at a tournament where the club has other teams.

The benefits of unifying your club include:

- **A sense of pride:** A strong colour palette will create a sense of pride within the club. The club will have its own community that is created if the colours and designs are strong and unique. A strong kit will make youngsters feel proud to represent their club, increasing confidence and therefore win rates.

- **Discipline:** The ritual of putting a kit on is almost a psychological warm-up for the training session or game day. The net result of wearing a uniform or kit will be improved discipline and concentration during training.

- **Brand identity:** By having a strong identity, your club will create a brand. When I supported Carla Paterson with Hatch Warren Tigers, we made sure the whole club would be playing in orange tiger-print dresses, and they had black and orange training kit. This identity was then represented in everything, from the website through to the marketing flyers.

- **Togetherness:** It's important that in tough moments on the pitch the players are united.

Something as simple as a kit unified by colour creates a subliminal message to the players that they are playing for the club together.

- **Confidence:** Never underestimate how much a unifying look for your club gives confidence to your own players, but also how this comes across to the opposition. At grassroots level, the margins can be gained easily by simple and small wins. Unifying your club and having a set kit for travel, training and competing will give your players increased confidence, which will reflect on the pitch.

Creating Kitmas

KITMAS *noun*

The annual festival celebrating the start of the new sporting season. Observed primarily in July or August. Coaches and players celebrate the new season by receiving new club kits.

(*also* **KITMAS TIME**) The period leading up to the start of the season, sporting a 'holy day' that celebrates a new season.

(*also* **KITMAS DAY**) The day when coaches and players celebrate the giving and receiving of new club kits.

At KitKing, we coined the term 'Kitmas' because James Cooling in our sales team, a former Derby FC player, recalled how he felt about receiving his kit when playing football professionally: 'It's like Christmas but in the summer.'

We now use 'Kitmas Day' to encourage clubs to place their order earlier in the year so they can get their kit for pre-season. If they give themselves time, they can create a Kitmas Day for their clubs.

I've worked with close to 100 professional clubs and national governing bodies. Most do not have a Kitmas Day. Their players are given their kit in a black bin-bag. What does that say about the club or organisation? How does it make the player feel?

Hollywood has produced many films, such as *The Mighty Ducks* (1992), *Cool Runnings* (1993) and *Coach Carter* (2005), about a ragtag bunch of players that have been built into a team by an unwitting coach. Each has a moment when the kit is unveiled as the turning point for the team's success. That moment of unification is the Kitmas moment when all divisions are forgotten about, the team come together and the players start to perform.

Grassroots and professional clubs alike can create a Kitmas Day. It needs some organisation, but the rewards for the effort will be there.

> **CASE STUDY: England's Kitmas Day**
>
> Kitmas Day is a special day if you are playing football for England before a tournament. In 2022, the FA took Kitmas Day to another level and invited Prince William to hand out the players' shirts for the men's World Cup.
>
> Every player received a presentation box from Prince William, starting with the captain, Harry Kane. The box contained a shirt with their number on it and a collage image of every previous player to wear that number at a World Cup. There was also a personal signed message to each player from the team manager, Gareth Southgate.
>
> It's possible to create an annual event for your club that has the flavour of England's Kitmas – although the scale might be a little smaller.

How to identify the best kit supplier and/or partner

Today, clubs are spoilt with options to outfit them. Global brands such as Nike, Adidas and Puma all have options to outfit clubs, while smaller companies will provide an unbranded option.

I've met hundreds of newly elected club chairs that will be headstrong on a particular brand, regardless of whether they are a suitable fit. Brands and suppliers go through cycles, just as sports teams do. It is therefore important to make sure you as a club review your kit offering every three to five seasons. Year one of a new brand will be the most challenging as everyone within the club will be moving over to the newly appointed brand/supplier.

What are the steps you need to take?

Apparel is an area we all use to identify ourselves; kit becomes highly emotional as we are removing the ability to have choice. Get this wrong and you will have members, players, fans and potentially the media holding you accountable.

- **Obtain quotes:** Any person within the club needs to make sure they get at least three quotes before recommending a kit partner; you are not only spending the club's funds but also club members' money. Price is only one factor in the choosing of a kit partner.

- **Make a criteria list:** To protect your decision making, do what the professionals do and consider a list of objective criteria that all stakeholders have bought into. Not every brand is suitable for your organisation. Make sure you focus on the needs and wants of your organisation rather than your personal choice as a consumer. Make sure you engage all areas of the club in this criteria list so that you can lead this process professionally with all parties in mind.

Price, cost, design and service levels are all key criteria, whether you are a grassroots or a professional club. There are also other criteria you may not have considered, which you can add depending on your situation. Either way, a criteria list offers a rational approach to appointing a new kit brand and supply partner. See this simple example below, and visit https://grassrootstogreatness.club for a full list of criteria.

- **Go out to tender:** If kit is a hot topic of discussion within your club, you're likely to be asked to go out to tender with your kit requirements. You have a reason for going out to tender; either your club is not happy with the current kit brand or it needs a refresh. It's likely you haven't done this for several years. You are now responsible for the attire of your entire organisation – a somewhat daunting thought if you get it wrong.

- **Weight the tender criteria:** Although I'm recommending a tender process, you will need to make sure you get the weighting criteria correct for your club. I would recommend you take some time meeting potential suppliers before you publish the actual requirements. Make sure you use this time to fact-find about the market.

What options do each of the potential partners have that might be relevant for your club? How can you make sure you weight the tender criteria in a manner that would have the members' needs at the heart of the final decision?

Criteria list examples

This is an example of some of the criteria you may wish to consider. Not all clubs are the same, so it's important for you to use suitable criteria to assess which suppliers satisfy the needs of your club. Weightings can be given to each supplier for the criteria chosen. Remember to consider all stakeholders when completing this task.

1. Commercials

- Price
- Commercial offer
- Gift of kit
- Added value
- Brand equity (cool factor and global appeal)
- Replica sales impact
- Training wear sales impact
- Leisurewear sales impact

2. Product Management

- Product quality (fabrics)
- Design

- Sustainable fabrics
- Cradle to grave evidence
- Forecasting programme
- Big and tall sizes
- Women's fit
- Kids' sizing
- Bespoke(ness)
- Minimum order quantity bespoke
- Product innovation
- Product USP (any additional USPs)

3. Ethical Trading

- Factory audit and ethical trading
- Environmental policy
- CO_2 policy

4. Service Levels

- Lead times/speed of service (bespoke)
- Sped of service (stock lines)
- Club management team

5. Marketing

- Social media marketing
- In store POS
- e-commerce support

6. Culture and Values

- Brand fit with club's values
- Brand values fit with club's players and fans

A full list of criteria is available on the website at http://grassrootstogreatness.club.

Top 10 things to think about when choosing a kit partner

KitKing works with grassroots through to professional sports clubs alongside national and global governing bodies who are at the end of their kit cycle to find their next kit brand. While we do this week in and week out, the chairs and commercial directors of professional clubs review their kit brand once every three to five years. That is long enough for the market to move on, and for what the brands have to offer to change.

The larger the brand, the less likely they are to partner with your club directly. Larger brands have a huge desire to partner with clubs; however, they are more likely to want to run the partnership via a strategic partner, such as KitKing. Smaller brands are more likely to work directly with clubs.

Here are ten top tips for sports clubs seeking kit partnerships.

1. Commercial offer

This is *always* the focus. However, price isn't everything. The best commercial kit partnerships are those where the brand adds value over and above cash or free kit.

Price is only one lever in any kit negotiation. What is your pain point? What can the brand offer you that may be of high value to you and not so much to them? You might think your club is not really of importance to the biggest brands in the world, but if you position your club well they will want to partner with you as much as you them.

CASE STUDY: Price is only one lever

The **German National Football (GNF)** federation chose **Adidas** over Nike in 2016 for a four-year contract from 2018 to 2022. The offer from Adidas was reportedly not as high as Nike's; however, Adidas promised to bring the manufacturing of the national jersey back to Germany, which was something that Nike could not offer.

During the 2020 Euros, Adidas also hosted the German national side on their campus in Herzogenaurach. The Adidas campus is surrounded by forest and is located 20km from the Nuremberg Airport, making it a fantastic venue for the national team to isolate, prepare and travel to games.

2. Sustainability

We hear on a number of occasions about brands that use recyclable fabrics and have a sustainable use policy. Here are some of the tricks we have seen brands play:

- Limiting the use of sustainable fabrics to a set number of products

- Transporting product in a unsustainable manner, eg flying goods in, as it takes a long time to manufacture goods using sustainable fabrics

If sustainability is important to you, dig into the details of the policy – don't just accept what you are told. Get the brands to prove their policies with factory reports, independent testing and auditing. They will all have this information if what they are pitching is true. The bigger the brand, the more likely their pitch is to be true, as most product claims would have to be verified by their legal departments. The smaller brands are the ones to watch out for. They can take risks and seek forgiveness after.

3. Service delivery

Smaller brands have fewer people and therefore can react faster. However, with fewer people there is more risk, eg an account manager will always go on holiday when you have an unexpected new player arrival. Larger brands may have more headcount, but they are more likely to go through a supply partner like KitKing.

CONSIDER:

- What is the response time for questions?
- Is there a target key performance indicator (KPI)?
- What's the delivery schedule from brand to club?

4. Partnership versus supplier

To have a 'supplier', the mindset is often: I win, you lose. To be a kit/apparel 'partner' is a win-win mindset.

Let's go back to the example of the GNF. When they started looking for a place for their national football team to live and train during the UEFA Euro 2020 tournament, they wanted a space that would bring their players together and unlock a great team dynamic. Adidas realised this was exactly the vision they had to further develop their state-of-the art internal campus. As partners, Adidas offered the new campus to the GNF. Adidas made sure that the

GNF was involved in every aspect of the build, from design through to development – every detail had the GNF at its heart.

Adidas essentially built a training stadium for the GNF, which was then repurposed post the Euros. Win-win all round, and when the kit deal is up for tender in 2022, the commercials might not just be the only consideration.

5. Brand recognition

Does the brand have an appeal to the key stakeholders of the club? Your key stakeholders are:

- Professional players
- Pathway/youth players
- Staff and executive team
- Supporters

Get one of these areas wrong at your peril. The complaints will end up in your inbox.

6. Price of goods

Is pricing of goods important to your stakeholders? Does your club need to be accessible?

What if a pathway / youth player can't afford their kit? Will the brand support these players?

7. Product quality

Some of the biggest brands in the world have messed up – everything from footballs bursting through to rugby players' shorts ripping.

How much is the club wanting to compromise on product quality? Is there a proven track record of product quality? The last thing you need is a commercial decision impacting players' performance.

8. Product innovation

Is there any product innovation you need to consider to give your players an edge?

9. The female offering

The explosion of female participation within sports is predicted to have exponential growth over the next three to five years. Where will your club be in that time frame? How will your kit partnership work over that period?

Most clubs are currently looking to increase female participation and attendance. Therefore, make sure the brand's offer is acceptable not just for the here and now but for the contract length.

10. Retail proposal

The retail offer for sports clubs is often overlooked or forgotten about. At a simplistic level, can the partnership provide:

- Products on-demand for store retail?
- An e-commerce offering (which they can service or execute)?

Depending on the club's capacity and capability, they may choose to outsource these.

Summary

A unified look while training and playing is essential in building professionalism and confidence on and off the pitch. Unified kit gives a sense of pride, discipline and brand identity. It can be used as a basis for meaningful rituals, like Kitmas Day.

This chapter also tells you how to choose a kit supplier, and key questions to ask.

CONSIDER:

- Does the club have a nominated kit officer?
- Does the kit officer have the skills to run a commercial process to identify the right partner?
- Has the kit officer got an agreed criteria list before the process starts in order to take all stakeholders along a journey?

7
Belonging

I t's human nature to want to belong to a social group. People can belong to several, starting with their family and moving on to primary or secondary school, university, sports clubs, Scouts or Guides, and church or religious groups. A sense of belonging comes when a group works towards a common goal. The ground staff that prepare your pitches celebrating when the team scores and the team thanking them for the work they have done throughout the year are all the small building blocks that create a sense of belonging. From having a positive atmosphere within a clubhouse after a set of fixtures through to club members wearing club leisurewear apparel, these are all steps towards that feeling of belonging.

The United Nations (UN) has now recognised the role of team sports and has stated that it is a clear human right to have access to sport. The United Nations Educational, Scientific and Cultural Organization (UNESCO) is a specialised agency of the UN, which is aimed at promoting world peace and security through international cooperation in education, arts, sciences and culture, including sport. Its International Charter of Physical Education, Physical Activity and Sport is 'a rights-based reference that orients and supports policy- and decision-making in sport. It promotes inclusive access to sport by all without any form of discrimination.'[26]

In 2015, the UN launched seventeen global Sustainable Development Goals (SDGs) to be achieved by 2030, which can be found at www.un.org/ sustainabledevelopment/sustainable-development-goals. Sport is linked to six of these:

- Good health and well-being (SDG 3)
- Quality education (SDG 4)
- Gender equality (SDG 5)
- Decent work and economic growth (SDG 8)
- Reduced inequalities (SDG 10)
- Partnerships (SDG 17)

Sport in itself provides great positivity for all. At a basic level, it offers fitness, teamwork and life skills.

High-level sports can influence change politically and culturally. A great example of this would be the stance that global athletes have taken on racism by taking the knee. Almost every sport around the world has joined forces with this movement and athletes have created a sense of belonging to the cause of fighting racism.

How do you know when you have created a sense of belonging?

If the C+L+U=B framework is followed, it's likely you will have the foundations for a sense of belonging.

It's well known that young people need inspiration and guidance from positive role models. Negative role models can lead them to turn to gangs or involve them in criminal activities that might result in them ruining their lives. Negative role models take the essence of the C+L+U=B framework to generate a detrimental outcome.

If we take the C+L+U=B framework and turn it into a positive, safe and family-friendly sports club environment, your club will create a huge sense of belonging. People from the local community, disadvantaged families and migrant communities should be able to fit in and thrive within it. If they are accepted and over a period begin to take on leadership positions, you will know your club has created a sense of belonging.

Other signs that members feel like they belong include them volunteering their time for club-related matters, be it coaching youngsters, serving drinks behind the bar or sweeping up the sheds. Members will vote with their feet and their time if they feel like they belong to the club. If they do not have that feeling, you will find that they simply do not support the club. If they do, they will urge their families and friends to get involved too.

Why don't people always feel like they belong?

When a few members within a club end up making most of the decisions, over a period, the power within these roles – if not held accountable by members – can start to turn sour. Committees that have an autocratic approach and don't listen to their members will not recognise the power they have, and most importantly the impact this has on their membership. A common trait of these poor committees is a lack of self-awareness. Leadership groups within a sports club can forget how much of a leadership role they have within the wider community. They themselves are often the reason as to why members do not feel like they belong to the club.

If you are part of a committee that you think might not be in touch with its membership, start asking honest questions of the members and noticing their behaviours. Do they feel a sense of belonging? Are they behaving as if they do? Maybe it's worth the leadership in your club taking a different approach to make more people feel included.

Sports clubs are built on passion, on those that think with their heart, not their head. That passion comes from the fans at the pro level and the volunteers at the grassroots level. The fans and volunteers feel as though the club is a part of who they are and it plays an important role in their lives. If the leadership of the club isolates the fans and volunteers or does not consult them on key decisions, there will naturally be a divide between the club and those that have that passion. Disrespect the fans and volunteers and you will lose that sense of belonging and therefore the foundation the club is built on. Get rid of the passion, you get rid of the heart and immediately lose that sense of belonging.

The obvious barriers to creating a sense of belonging are the 'isms': racism, sexism, ageism. Clubs should state in their policies that they have zero tolerance towards any behaviour promoting one of these barriers.

The biggest barrier is something that often goes unnoticed and is not spoken about: a lack of money can prevent players getting involved with a club. Make sure your club sets aside provisions to support those that want to join in but can't due to financial pressures. From discounted fees or subs through to donated kit and equipment, you can make changes to allow those from lower socio-economic backgrounds to join your club.

Items of belonging

My garage is filled with large bags of kit. After culling several times, I'm still left with about five bags of items that I'll always treasure. Many other team sports athletes are the same.

I spent some time digging into why these garments meant so much to me. I realised they fall into three categories: garments that are earned, nostalgic pieces or items that I identify with the club or organisation.

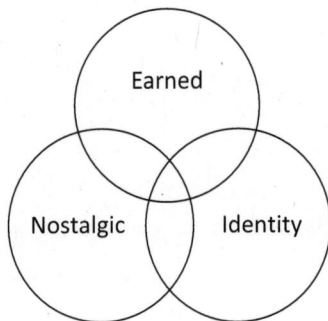

Earned items

Earned items are pieces of kit that are gifted by the club for achievement of a milestone by the athlete. Examples include:

- Cap – debut selection
- Ball – five-wicket haul or hat trick
- 100 caps

The earned item itself is as important as the person who presents it to the athlete. It represents a significant achievement for the athlete and allows them to reflect on the hard work they have put in and the people that have helped them to reach that milestone. The athlete is not only recognised by their peers and juniors within the club or team, but the coaches and seniors within the organisation. By presenting an earned item, no doubt the athlete will gain a level of pride and humility. My own earned items are my first men's team kit and the cap I wore on debut for Loughborough University.

Yorkshire cricket players have two levels of achievement to gain, so they are always striving for the next 'earned item'. The items they can earn are:

1. **Second team capped player:** All kit with white rose in bud

2. **Full county capped player:** All kit with white rose in full bloom

I was fortunate to work with Yorkshire for about three years and one thing that struck me was how important it was for junior players to get their hands on a full county Yorkshire cap. This may have a direct correlation to Yorkshire being one of the clubs that has produced the most number of players for England.

There is no set rule about how you become a fully capped player; it is decided by a hierarchy within the club.

On some occasions, the player has played for England before he has come back and received his full county cap. The hunger and desire to achieve this earned item is deeply engrained into the culture of the club.

CONSIDER:

- What does a player get from your club on debut?
- What does the club give the player on playing at the highest level?
- What other milestones might be awarded within your club?

CASE STUDY: A record-breaking cap from a very special captain

James Anderson, England cricket's record-breaking fast bowler, was capped for the 150th time in December 2019 at the Boxing Day test at the Centurion Park ground, South Africa. He joins an elite group of players to achieve this milestone and is the only fast bowler on this list.

His first captain **Nasser Hussain** who presented his first cap was asked to present his 150th cap, which came as a complete surprise to Anderson. Hussain gave an emotionally charged speech and said: '150 test matches for any cricketer is special, 150 test matches as a fast bowler is an unbelievable achievement, well done James Anderson.'[27]

Anderson, later reflecting on the moment and career milestone, acknowledged the role that Hussain played in his career: 'It meant a lot to me receiving it from my first captain who showed faith in me all those years ago.'[28]

Anderson's cap was a record-breaking milestone for any player, but he is a fast bowler and managed to keep himself fit for close to twenty years. His item of belonging will mean a lot to him; however, the ECB recognise it was just as important to consider who gave the item to him. By asking Hussain, his first captain and the person who gave that confidence, trust and faith in a young fast bowler, it not only shows how much Hussain is proud of Anderson's achievement but it will also show the wider squad that they have this milestone to achieve if they work hard. One day, it will be natural for Anderson in turn to give a cap to a player that might break his record.

Nostalgic items

Nostalgic items evoke a memory of success, happiness or struggle by a player. The nature of team sports means you will be spending long periods of time with your teammates. The time spent with each other is escalated on a tour. Tours are competitive and social trips that will evoke memories for years to come.

Examples of nostalgic items:

- Finals shirt

- Shirt worn playing at a 'once in a lifetime' venue, eg Wembley Stadium

- Tour shirt

- First bat

- First captain's armband

CASE STUDY: Sock it to them

In rugby, the **Barbarian FC** are a touring team built to entertain fans. Over 130 years old, the team is selected from all parts of the world to play exhibition matches globally. The club colours are black and white and the jersey design is hooped – an original identity in world rugby. The Barbarians play against international teams; the games are competitive and watched by full-capacity crowds. Playing for Barbarian FC is one of the highest honours in world rugby; some deem it as prestigious as playing for their country.

The Barbarians have two traditions that are unique to them. First, they will select a player who is uncapped (has not played internationally) and portrays all the Barbarians' and rugby values. Second, every player wears the socks of their first grassroots club or school. Most players will wear both.

Why is this important? For the player, it's a chance to share their identity at the highest level. Their first club men's kit or 1st XV kit would be an 'earned' item. When wearing their club or school socks while playing for the Barbarians, the players are given a chance to reflect on their journey through to the highest level of rugby. The club socks also inspire the next generation from within those clubs and schools, showing that the journey is made possible by those who have gone before them.

Identity items

As humans we are a species that socialise; we all long to feel a sense of belonging to a tribe. This tribe could be as simple as your family, in modern day terms, it could be your school, college, university or sports club.

Thousands of years ago, the tribe would have been location based, ie your village or your clan. The first known form of human identity was over 100,000 years ago with jewellery. This was used to identify a combination of status within tribes, and also which tribe they might be part of. About 10,000 years ago in China, we see the first examples of tattoos being used as a form of identity. Tattoos were used to mark and identify prisoners. A great example of tattoos being used to identify as part of a tribe comes from the Māoris, the indigenous people of New Zealand. Māoris did not have a written language prior to meeting Europeans, they would use their facial tattoos to identify themselves to other tribes. These tattoos were called Mokos; no two were the same. They all had symbols and marks telling stories of their families, locations and tribes. As humans started to wear clothes, tribal garments in specific colours were an increasingly important factor in identify. Humans would find pigments in nature and dye their clothes to signify a level of identity towards a tribe. As sophisticated methods of dyeing prints emerged, tribes used these methods to create unique identities.

Items of identity within a sports club have a functional role on pitch. The shirt, shorts and socks are worn in clear colourways to allow players to identify each other, but also to allow referees and fans to identify individual players.

What about outside of the court or pitch? What garments are used to identify as part of a 'tribe'?

In modern day terms, we can find garments being used to create a form of identity everywhere we look. Sports clubs, college and universities, political parties and even street gangs are where the most prevalent items of identity still play a huge role. Two of the most prevalent gangs in Los Angeles USA, the Crips (blue) and the Bloods (red) have clear items of identity. The bandana being the garment, the colour signifying which gang (or tribe) they belong to.

Football, rugby, golf, cricket, hockey clubs alongside traditional educational institutes each have garments with striking and unique designs that are worn as items of identification.

Blazer and jackets

The very first blazer can be traced back to Cambridge and Oxford cricket and rowing clubs in the 1820s.[29] Blazers were not dinner jackets, they were sports jackets, and over time have become an item of belonging.

They were devised with two things in mind; identity and functionally, to be worn for warmth on cold mornings. Designed in strikingly bright colours with stripes, patterns or braids to garishly stand out. They were initially spotted on Henley on Thames, and very soon were worn by the athletes on dry land.

If we fast forward to 1950s America, we see a casual garment with similar functional requirement being worn by college and club athletes. Dubbed the Letterman Jacket, they were initially used to identify student athletes around campus, but soon moved to becoming a garment that was earnt.

One of the most famous blazers in global sports is both earnt and an item of identity. The famous emerald, green blazer worn by the winner of the Masters. For over eighty years, the green blazer has been a symbol of being part of an elite tribe of golfers to have either won one of the most prestigious golfing competitions, the Masters, or be an Augusta National club member. It is both an item of identity and an item that has been earnt.

Ties

Neck ties have a similar history to blazers. Traditional sports clubs have fashioned garish designs to create a clear identity. One of the most famous sports ties is that of the Marylebone Cricket Club (MCC), the original cricket club in the world. Nobody is 100% clear of the origins of the MCC tie in yellow and orangey red (famously known as the egg and bacon colours).[30] Members proudly adorn this tie during the summer fixtures at the home of the MCC, Lords Cricket Ground in St Johns Wood London. Some also wear an egg and bacon blazer. The MCC generally sit within the pavilion and are undoubtably a tribe. As a member myself, I've travelled to and from games on the train or tube. Almost every time I've been stopped by a member of the public to ask me about the game, or how I earned the tie.

Both examples are quite traditional and are very male focused. Modern day sport is far more inclusive and as fashion moves away from blazers and ties, we are likely to see a change in these items of identity.

Consider:

- What items of identity does your club have?

- How can athletes aspire to achieve them?

- How can members and athletes identify as part of the club 'tribe'?

- Is there a striking colour palette or design that clearly identifies your club?

- Are the items provided inclusive for male and females?

Loughborough till I die

I've been fortunate to be part of some great sporting institutions and I still have a great sense of belonging long after I've stopped being a player. Loughborough University was a community in and of itself. In my time, there were eighteen halls of residences on campus, each with an individual identity, but they all became irrelevant when representing or supporting the university.

One of the key social gatherings was the 'sing off'. Every hall would compete against each other at the students' union building in a football or rugby match style sing off. After an hour of chanting at the top of our voices, the president would thank everyone and start a rendition of 'Loughborough Till I Die'. The halls that had moments before been competing against each other now all sang in unison a song that shed the individual hall identity, which brought each person together as part of the 'Loughborough family' in that moment.

The university's sport at the time was run and organised by the students. In fact, on my university team kit, the logo is Loughborough Students, not Loughborough University. The sports were run *by* the students, *for* the students. The university staff were there to support, in particular at the elite level. What did this do? It grew leaders.

I was fortunate enough to be a member of the cricket club committee from 2002 to 2006. In 2005 we won the Athletic Union Sports Club of the Year, due to our leadership. My sense of belonging to Loughborough came from the successful combination of the C+L+U=B parts. I bleed purple. Loughborough till I die!

Summary

We have gone through the history of sports clubs and the C+L+U=B framework. We have explored how to make a club successful, defined by a sense of belonging, not necessarily by virtue of on-field performances. We have identified key areas for you to review and improve on using the theory.

You can use the theory to reflect upon your club and other clubs. Identify areas of improvement and what other clubs might be doing better to create a sense of belonging.

CONSIDER:

- Do you think your club has a sense of belonging?
- Can you introduce items of belonging next session?
- Is there a true identity that all stakeholders can belong to?

PART THREE
THE 5 PS

Now we are going to explore the five Ps – or five pillars – that underpin the C+L+U=B framework.

1. Profile

It is so important to consider the profile of the club. How are you perceived by the opposition, locals and potential new players?

Can they even find you online? I am shocked at how many clubs do not have a website and are reliant on Facebook pages or Instagram to communicate. I know of several clubs that have over 150 players yet have no online profile, meaning they are missing potential new players and coaches that move to the local area.

2. Philosophy

Successful clubs have a style of play that reinforces their brand. When working on Hatch Warren Tigers with Carla (see Chapter 5), we talked at length about the style of play she wanted. Within other sports, such as cricket, rugby and football, clubs will have a style of play that is bought into by coaches and players. Examples such as the All Blacks, England Cricket (Bazball) and Barcelona FC (Tiki-taka) can be brought into grassroots clubs.

3. Partnerships

This covers all partnerships a club will require – everything from local businesses to the local council to schools.

4. Place (pitch/court/premises)

A large percentage of clubs do not own their own premises and are sporting nomads. Newly formed clubs, in particular women's and girls' clubs, really do struggle to get access to a regular place to train and play. How can your club get a regular place? Who do you need to speak to? How can you get more access to more time?

We will explore how to get the right 'place' where you can train, compete and socialise, or if you have a place already, how to make the most of it.

5. People

Clubs are people-centric organisations. This P is exploring all the leadership roles in a sports club and the types of people that typically take them on. This section is particularly important, not only to identify potential new recruits but also to allow you to reflect on your own committee to identify behaviour that might not be in the best interests of the wider club.

In the following chapters, I'll unpack the five Ps for you.

8
Profile

You are what Google says you are. Have you ever Googled your own club? Have you tried to work out what a new player might come across if they moved into your area and wanted to find a sports club?

Whether your club is a start-up or is well established, it's important to have a clear online presence. With so many platforms and forms of communication, your club needs a digital strategy. It doesn't need to be complex, but it will make clear the role of each channel and who is responsible for it.

Team managers place orders for kit, balls and equipment for their particular teams or clubs with KitKing every day. As part of the account opening procedure, account managers will naturally try to find out more about the clubs by Googling them. It astounds me how often clubs do not have a digital footprint. They are missing a huge trick.

The physical aspect of a club profile is just as important, and clubs are notoriously forgetful about it. As a cricketer (playing in a pre- and post-Google Maps era), I cannot tell you how often I would go to away games and not be able to find the entrance or the ground itself. Sometimes the car park would be in a different location to the club, or certain games would not be held at the home ground and there would be a secondary site not mentioned on a club's website. I would find this out the hard way. Clubs assume they are catering for just their own members; they forget about the external stakeholders and what value these bring. Perhaps an opposition player is looking to move clubs – what impression does the lack of visibility give to them?

Have you thought about what new members might experience when joining your club? How would new players, young players and their parents feel? How does your offer compare with another club they might go to?

How your profile attracts players

Players who want to move clubs for whatever reason but are staying local are clearly going to think about which club they enjoy playing at and which delivers the best experience.

My first club from the age of twelve to twenty-eight was Old Chelmsfordians. When I came to realise I needed to change, I had a number of options as I was well known in the local area. On the last Sunday of the season, I played and captained against Billericay Cricket Club in a friendly fixture. It had not previously crossed my mind to join that club, but the people and the facilities were fantastic – first impressions count. The club was well signposted throughout the town, with a clear sign at the entrance. There were also signs showing where to park. I had *never* experienced this before.

Over tea, the captain and I had a great conversation about the club. He highlighted their vision and where their areas of improvement were. The biggest focus at that time was their junior section, which was non-existent, having only about twenty-five players. It was clearly a well-organised club and, given that I was a coach, I could see I could add value. We lost the fixture, yet Billericay realised that we had several juniors who were there for development reasons. The first team players (some of whom are now pros) were talented and ended up coaching our youngsters throughout the game.

Over the next few weeks, I went online and researched the club and the people within it. I studied the website and spoke to a good amount of people. The physical and digital profiles were linked. My impression of the club remained the same; in fact, having such a well-run website upped my interest in them, especially after a such a pleasant playing experience.

I received a phone call from the first team captain and a committee member within a few weeks, and by the October I had made my mind up. I played and coached for Billericay Cricket Club for eight years. I played in the second team and supported the junior development coaches. I coached a number of age groups on Friday nights, ran one-to-one coaching sessions over the weekends and also coached summer camps. Many of the junior players then are now young men playing in the first team. In the last few years, I was proud to support an exceptionally driven mum to set up the women's and girls' section too. The junior section is now close to 250 players.

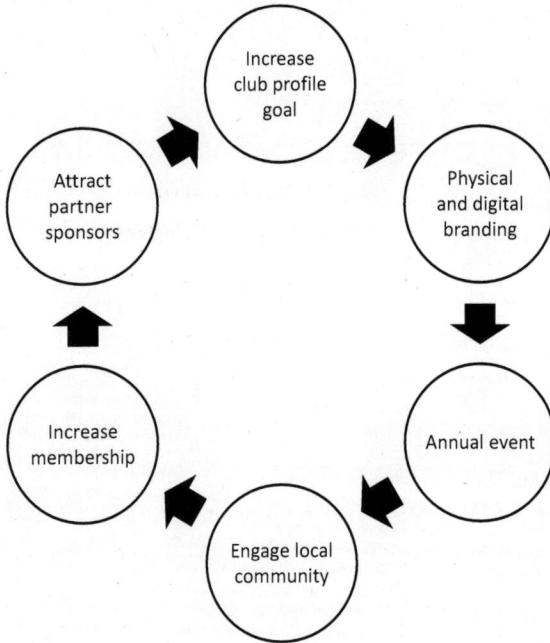

Increase club profile goal

Physical and digital branding

Annual event

Engage local community

Increase membership

Attract partner sponsors

If the digital profile, the practicalities of finding the club and the experience of meeting and being welcomed by players had not been good, I would possibly have not joined.

Creating a good website

Every club needs a smart, professional website so that once people have located you via word of mouth or digital searches, they are impressed with what they learn and see. Make sure you are critical about how you portray your club in order not to isolate anyone. Be inclusive and reflect diversity in your images throughout the site.

There are various platforms to host your website. I recommend Pitchero (www.pitchero.com), Teamer (www.teamer.net), HitsSports (www.hitssports. com), Plai (www.plai.io) and Heja (https://heja.io) for sports clubs. They're all slightly different, so it's worth comparing their features and benefits. There is also information about this on my website, https:// grassrootstogreatness.club.

If you're a small grassroots club, you might want to use a simple platform like Wix (www.wix.com) to get going and get better.

Why is it so important to have a website?

1. It makes you easy to find

A high-quality, regularly updated website is crucial for any club. It's where the current membership and opposition can find basic information and the first port of call for potential new members.

Test up to ten different Google searches that people might type in to find you. Things like: 'What's my local football club?', 'Where can I play cricket?', 'Tennis clubs near me'. If you're not happy with your ranking, try to change it by tweaking your keywords.

Make sure your address, a popular search, is linked to Google Maps. If the venue for matches changes, update the listing for that week. Be easy to find, even for people who don't know you.

CONSIDER:

- What types of searches are relevant for your club?
- Where and how can you improve your ranking for obvious searches within your area?

2. It improves your credibility

A good-looking, up-to-date website will always improve your image to prospective players, coaches, parents and volunteers. The website is the shop window of the club; it's the best way of building credibility and trust to attract future players.

Remember, location might not be the only reason to join your club. It's likely future players, parents, coaches and volunteers will review a few clubs in the area. Make sure you've removed any barriers to contacting your club. Include a welcoming page that includes all areas of the club, outlines your vision and introduces the key people.

3. It improves your communication

A 'contact us' page with a form or a set of emails will allow members and prospective members to reach the key members of the club. Social media tools, for example WhatsApp groups, Facebook groups and X, will also be a good way to communicate with the current membership. Remember, social media is moving at a fast pace, and different age groups spend time on different social media sites. You will need to assess which is the best method for your membership.

4. It reduces volunteer time

The specialist platforms mentioned above such as Pitchero and HitsSports are a great tool to reduce volunteers' time. One of the most frustrating tasks a captain and selection committee has is selecting players for fixtures. Knowing who is available is a task in itself. For a club with a smaller membership, Heja is a good free app that can be used for selection.

5. It attracts new players and members

You never know who is looking and who will be interested. After I graduated, I went to play cricket in Australia for a season. It was 2006 and I had a BlackBerry as the iPhone still hadn't been released. I jumped on to Google and found a club and academy in Brisbane that was perfect. I immediately reached out via the 'contact us' page. A few emails and some late-night phone calls later, I joined Redland Tigers Cricket Club in Brisbane.

6. It improves club finances (and saves time)

One of the most frustrating tasks every club has is collecting annual membership fees and match fees for each player. I've heard every excuse under the sun from, 'I've not got cash on me; can I pay you next week?' through to, 'I thought as I'm a student I didn't need to pay.'

Many specialist digital platforms allow you to either automate payment collection through your website or collect payments via contactless methods. This not only means the club's cashflow gets better immediately, but volunteers are not wasting time chasing players for payment or nagging them to set up standing orders.

7. It attracts partners and sponsors

The better the digital presence of your club and the stronger the website, the more people will have you on their radar. Clearly, being in the local news will also raise the profile of the club. In turn, this will result in attracting sponsors, partners and benefactors.

Other ways to raise your profile

E-newsletters

Monthly e-newsletters are a fantastic way of sharing good news with your membership. Don't make the communication too frequent as people can get bored, but too infrequent will make members lose interest. Make sure the content is fun, relevant and shares positivity about the club as a whole.

As your club grows, you may have multiple sites and days of the week in which different parts of the club train and play. Therefore, the news of the U9s winning a streak of fixtures might not be as well known to the wider membership as the men's first team news.

Social media

Facebook, X, TikTok, Instagram and YouTube are all great content hosts to keep your membership engaged and to drive traffic back to your website. Social media can be time-consuming to manage, but there is a lot of free software out there that can make the social media volunteer's life a lot easier.

These free software management tools for social media are great for a number of reasons:

- Post management (scheduling posts)
- Designing graphic posts
- Creating video posts (short- to medium-length videos)

Software such as Pitchero allows automatic posting of content to various channels.

Make sure you think about the role of each platform for the club. Remember, different age groups will use different channels.

CONSIDER:

- Does your club have a social media policy?

Local or national media

Your club will, on occasion, have a newsworthy story: a player achieves something out of the ordinary – maybe a club, local or even national record – or some other good news story. Something simple as a record number of juniors signed up for the season is a news story that local press will be interested in. Make sure you have a process set up in advance for this event.

CONSIDER:

- Do you know any local journalists?
- What kind of stories are they looking for?

What assets do you need to create?

Branding and brand guidelines

This sounds very official. Why might a grassroots club need a set of brand guidelines? Most people associate a brand with a logo, but a brand is far more than that. The brand is everything from a core set of values to the tone of voice you use in communication and how your coaches deliver their sessions.

A brand cannot be built overnight; it takes time and consistency. Start with a set of brand guidelines. This is especially important for a club that is tired and needs a refresh, or a start-up club. Sit down with the key stakeholders within the club to unearth the core brand and identity based on the C+L+U=B framework. This is closely linked to our next P, playing philosophy.

Get all your stakeholders to answer these questions:

- How do we want people to feel on the way in and out of our club? What experience would we like to give them?

- How do we want to be represented by our players, coaches and parents?

- What values do we want our players to uphold and coaches to embed?

- What life lessons might we bring to our players that are wider than the sport?

Don't be surprised if you find this difficult, as it's like looking at your club with a magnifying glass. Everything becomes bigger and seems problematic, but the problems can be turned into opportunities.

Once you have answers, you should be able to start working on the mission statement of the club. This mission, combined with the logo, will create the brand.

Turn all this work into a set of images and graphics. I would recommend the following:

- Mission, values and purpose, ie the story of your brand

- Logo lock up (do's and don'ts for the use of the logo)

- Colour palette

- Typography

- Tone of voice

Finally, get the brand mocked up on the kit. This always gets the biggest reaction. The right kit brand alongside your club logo will have an impact on the wider club. Publish an image of the mocked-up kits to everyone in the club, get feedback and take that feedback on board.

Brochures, flyers and posters

The majority of people in the local area will not have heard of your club, and if they have heard about it, they will not know about everything you offer. A physical brochure can work wonders. Local shops and supermarkets are still places where families will go a few times a week for their groceries. Highlight the club there with physical brochures, flyers and posters that are on brand. You can create digital versions too, which can be downloaded from your website.

You can create these items yourself on Canva or ask a volunteer to do it. If this is not an option you can find

a freelance designer on websites like Fiverr (www.
fiverr.com) or Peopleperhour (www.peopleperhour.
com). Make sure you have all your content ready and
be clear with the brief. If the brief is poor, the results
will also be poor.

Photography and videography

You don't need to pay for expensive professional pho-
tographers. Many of your members probably have
smartphones with powerful cameras. Ask the membership for their images for the website, brochure, etc,
and see what you get back. You will be surprised. The
ground staff might get to the club early or late on in
the day when the sun is rising or setting. They may
have some stunning photos. If they don't, ask them to
take some.

Video content can be a little more tricky because
editing is time-consuming. Again, I would recommend commissioning a video editor via Fiverr or
Peopleperhour. Send them the videos and make sure
the brief is clear. They will work wonders.

The only area of caution is making sure that people
are comfortable with their image being used. Ask permission, and get parents of children to put permission
in writing.

Annual events

Clubs that have raised their profile often have a head-line annual event, which is not sports-related and tends to be a fundraiser for the club. Other events are social gatherings with long-standing traditions attached to them. With every club I've been part of, this annual event is a fixture in the diary and a high-light of the year when volunteers, members, parents and players come together.

> **CASE STUDY: Raising money with a bang**
>
> **Nigel Kinch**, chair of **Sileby Town Cricket Club** in Leicestershire, set up an annual fireworks event in around 2000 – a big fundraiser to mitigate flood damage expenses. The club's ground is on the floodplain of the River Soar, and every year the ground and clubhouse would get flooded. The club would then use its reserves to renovate the damage – eventually, the clubhouse was built 1.5m above the ground.
>
> I played a season there in 2002 while I was a student at Loughborough University and heard the vision set out by Nigel. He wanted a thriving junior section, best-in-class facilities and a first team that would consistently be in the top three in the Leicestershire Premier League.
>
> Two decades later, the club has two pitches, multiple nets and a thriving junior, women's and girls' section. The first team is consistently up there in the league, as per Nigel's vision. Yet they still have to account for the flooding problem every year.

Over the years, the club has built its reserves through strong leadership, good financial planning and Nigel's natural entrepreneurial spirit. The fireworks night is key to this. The club sells tickets through local businesses and their Pitchero website. They advertise via posters, flyers and word of mouth.

Sileby Town CC's profile is raised, not just within the cricketing community but within Sileby itself. They attract a wider demographic to the club, which has increased their participation numbers. As the club's profile has gained traction over the years, they have now close to twenty-five local sponsors, and their headline kit sponsor is the local Kia dealership. I'm certain the Nigel of 2000 would never have believed the club would gain this much local support.

Summary

Even if you're a long-established club, your profile will almost certainly need to be dragged into the digital age so you can communicate effectively with members and the outside world to attract new talent. It's essential to invest in your website – they can be relatively cheap to create or update. You will also need good-quality print materials and a system for gathering social media content.

Your brand guidelines need to be created or revisited with all stakeholders. If your vision is not clear, it will become obvious.

Finally, a showstopper annual event with a reach beyond the club can raise funds and become a high-light in the community year, which automatically raises your club's profile.

CONSIDER:

- How can you start discussions among the leadership about your brand?
- What annual event could you start that brings the community together?

9

Philosophy: Playing, Club Culture And Ethos

A sports club is an organisation, similar to a company. It requires a mission in order to make sure it's not a ship without a sail and map. I have already highlighted the multiple stakeholders of a sports club: boards, committees, parents, players, fans and coaches. Professional clubs will also have paid staff.

All these people will have their own view of the club. They will come from various cultural backgrounds and have different beliefs. More than likely, they will have a varying degree of passion and emotion towards the club.

Think about the following questions:

- How do you get the entire organisation pulling in the same direction?

- How do you identify what is unique about your club?

- How do you make sure all the stakeholders adhere to the club's expectations?

- How do you make sure you bottle the magic formula of the club and ensure the formula lasts for future generations?

The answer: a club philosophy.

The three components of a club philosophy

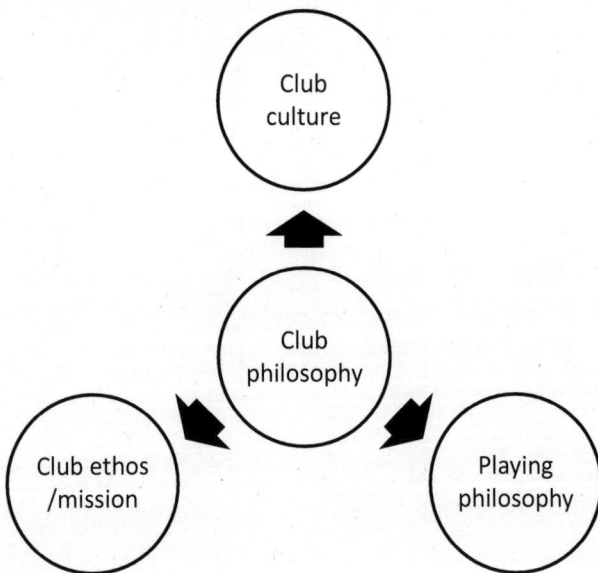

For me, a club philosophy is built of three components:

1. **Club culture**
   - How do we treat each other?
   - What do we want the opposition to say about us?
   - What do people say about the club when we are not in the room?

2. **Club ethos/mission**
   - Who are we?
   - What do we stand for?
   - What do we want to achieve?
   - Where are we going?

3. **Playing philosophy**
   - How do we want to play (eg, style)?
   - How do we coach our players?
   - How do they think under pressure (the winning moment)?
   - How do we link the above to technical, tactical, physical and mental attributes and skills needed?

If your club is a start-up, you will have a clean slate to create a philosophy and culture based on what you think is the correct direction. If you have an existing club, you will sit in one of two camps: either a club that is performing at its best or one that had success in its past. If you are in that success phase, how do you maintain and improve? If you had past glory, how do you find that magic again?

If you haven't created your club philosophy yet, do it. If you have already created it, revisit it and see where the club is versus what the document says.

What defines success?

From simply fielding a side to selecting as many players as possible, from giving playing experiences to young players to learn about game time to winning trophies, success can be defined in a number of ways by different clubs. It's therefore of paramount importance to clearly define what the philosophy of the club is, document it and drill down into what this looks like per team and age group.

For example, an aspiring dad who is a part-time coach of the U9s might define success as 'winning', but this response is more about the dad than the players. The U9s team are clearly only a few years into their playing careers and need development. Let's think about how many minutes of playing time a nine-year-old girl might have had if she started playing football at aged seven:

Approx. 20 games per season × 100 mins per game
= 2,000 mins = 33 hours and 33mins

The dad will be expecting the nine-year-old to have learnt the craft in less than one working week, spread out over two years. How can we help him understand that development is the key target, not winning every game?

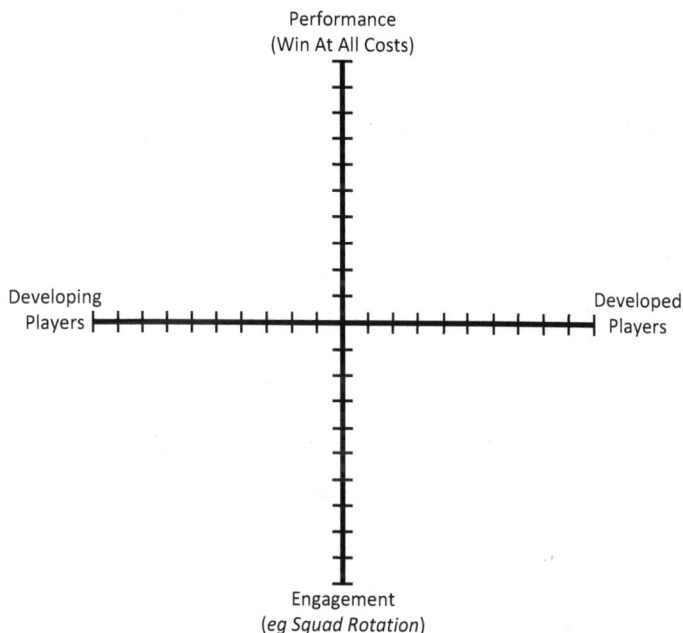

```
                    Performance
                   (Win At All Costs)

                         |
                         |
                         |
                         |
                         |
Developing               |                    Developed
Players  |——+—+—+—+—+—+—+—+—+—+—+—+—+—+—|     Players
                         |
                         |
                         |
                         |
                         |
                    Engagement
                   (eg Squad Rotation)
```

Creating a playing philosophy

Playing philosophy in football is very much about a style of play on-pitch during games. For me, this is relevant at the performance end of sports clubs. It's important for all sports clubs to establish a club culture that develops all types of characters and behaviours that form part of the club, regardless of whether you are about winning performances or engagement. A philosophy is set to make sure everyone adheres to the style of behaviours expected for the club or organisation. If people do not fit the mould, then they will recognise that the organisation is not for them based on this documentation.

To form a playing philosophy for the club:

1. Define the vision and mission statement.

2. Identify the core values.

3. Work on your philosophy. Are you producing only top talent and high performers or are you more focused on the development or social and engagement aspect of your club? Or are you doing both?

By analysing the club down to its core values, you will arrive at a statement and some guiding principles, which will create clarity among all stakeholders. If positioned in the right way, the leaders of all stakeholder groups will need to buy into, adhere and enforce the philosophy.

What happens when you create a strong club philosophy?

In business, companies have a vision, mission and purpose statement. A sports club philosophy is essentially the same. The big difference is that grassroots sports clubs are predominately run by passion-fuelled volunteers, whereas businesses have paid members of staff. Clubs have less contact time with their stakeholders than businesses, and therefore must be ten times more effective at communicating.

Rome wasn't built in a day, and it will take a few years to see the results of the work, so patience is key. Little success stories are all part of the journey of the club moving in the right direction. Accept lessons will be learnt and make sure any failures are embraced throughout the club. Remove subjectivity on how the club will be training, playing and socialising. Parents, players and coaches buying into the philosophy will result in everyone singing from the same hymn sheet.

How does a club philosophy line up with a playing philosophy?

Coaches' profiles and behaviour

Principles of play
• Club style of play
• Individual skills

Recruitment/ scouting policy

Playing philosophy

Youth development policy

Club mission

The playing philosophy of the club has to be led by the head coach or manager. In 2014, Gareth Southgate, the England national team manager, created the 'England DNA', the term used for 'club England' to play a style of football. This would mean all age groups, men's, women's and ability teams, would have a set vision laid out by the England manager as to what brand of football England play.

The 'England DNA' refers to the core principles, playing style and playing philosophy that is unique to the England teams. It represents the identity, values and characteristics that all stakeholders need to portray. Coaches and players can move around 'club England' and understand the DNA.

The five core elements of the England DNA[31] are as follows:

1. **Who we are:** The culture and values of the team.

2. **How we play:** Playing philosophy in and out of possession.

3. **The future England player:** Required skills and attributes of each player.

4. **How we coach:** Coaching style during training and on match day.

5. **How we support:** Both physical and psychological support is given.

Clearly, this philosophy related to the highest level of football. How do you turn this framework into something that is relevant for your club?

> ## CASE STUDY: More than a club
>
> In January 1968, the then newly elected club president, **Narcís de Carreras**, declared **FC Barcelona**, 'Més que un club' (more than a club).[32] This statement was the starting point of a newly found vision for Barcelona, which already had one of the largest club memberships in the world and owned its own stadium.
>
> Little did Carreras know at the time the power of this statement. The club has become a symbol of Catalan culture and an icon of national pride and this statement recognises the level of importance the club has within the Catalan culture.
>
> A decade later, the next president carried forward the 'more than a club' motto. This new regime saw the appointment of Dutchman Johann Cruyff, a former player, as first team coach. Cruyff quickly won games and trophies and won the hearts of the Catalans. He brought with him a strict playing philosophy dubbed 'Total Football'. Total Football is an attractive to watch, attacking style of play where players do not have set positions. The key is to keep possession of the ball and have as many shots as possible. Any outfield player should be able to move positions with any teammates.
>
> This clear playing philosophy was brought into the first team and results were quick to come in. Soon after, Cruyff recognised the playing philosophy could be

translated down into the reserves, academy and youth pathway, resulting in successful transition of players when injuries in the first team came around. When Cruyff was appointed, the club had poor attendance, no identity and huge financial debts. His playing philosophy quickly translated to results, and the attractive style play captivated supporters once again. Cruyff managed a golden age within Barcelona, winning multiple leagues and cups domestically and within Europe.

Cruyff manage to capture the imagination of hearts and minds around the world, and in an era of broadcasting, Barcelona started to draw eyeballs to watch this attractive football all the way round the world. To this day the playing philosophy remains, and Barcelona is one of the most supported and watched clubs globally due to the playing philosophy legacy Cruyff left the club with.

The benefits of a club philosophy

Creating a great club culture

It's imperative to link all the teams via a culture to achieve success as a club. There is a slight difference in team culture versus club culture. A great set of teams make a great overall club. In business, there is no point in having one department that has a great culture and performs in accordance with the vision of the company if all the other departments are under-performing. I believe the same principle applies to club culture.

Increasing purpose-based training

Players go through a playing journey and development cycle. Training that is not structured or part of a bigger philosophy will inevitably be a waste of time.

As a coach myself, I'm a big believer in practice with purpose. If your club has twenty-five teams, the club will have twenty-five coaches and therefore twenty-five different methods of training. Those coaches will be training at different times of the week and therefore there won't be an overall approach for the club. A shared vision and strategy is needed to help players and coaches form part of the overall organisation. Having an agreed style of play or a methodology that is taught throughout different age groups will result in club players rather than team players.

Documenting clear mission and values

A major part of the club philosophy is creating a documented mission and core values. This document is the foundation of everything the club stands for.

CONSIDER:

- Who are you?
- What do you believe in?
- How do you operate?
- What are the behaviours of the club?

- Are you a club that wants to lift trophies, a club that is all about player development or a club that is all about engagement – or a combination of all three?

If you have a clearly defined mission and set of values, your club will have a clear foundation for the future.

Providing clarity for parents, coaches and players

The more people you have involved in your club and the larger the organisation becomes, the more differences of opinion are likely to occur. A philosophy will remove subjectivity and any areas of doubt.

A club philosophy will bind together the club vision and overall mission, values and culture. This is so important for all club coaches or managers to buy into. Take parents through these areas at the beginning of each season to get their buy-in. Bring in the players after the parents: if they are aged under fourteen, it's unlikely they will be able to understand the overall philosophy. Try to break it down to a simple set of achievable behaviours.

Establishing a code of conduct or behaviour

The club philosophy will identify a code of conduct or behaviour. The players represent the club and a hot-headed player that confronts referees or umpires will not be tolerated by most clubs.

How poor behaviour is dealt with is important as the opposition will see and hear about how matters are handled. A philosophy that makes a code of conduct clear will mean the coach or manager has a clear set of principles to fall back on. The consequences of poor behaviour are therefore not a personal choice but are made by the club.

One of the best examples of a code of conduct is that of Manchester United under Sir Alex Ferguson. He made it clear that all players were to turn up to matches in club suits. This created a sense of discipline and unification prior to matches throughout his era.

Building a legacy

Once created, a successful philosophy will last generations. Regardless of coaches, captains or players, the All Blacks philosophy has lived on for over fifty years. FC Barcelona is another organisation with a non-negotiable philosophy – to change the 'Barcelona way' would be sacrilege.

Summary

A club philosophy binds together the club vision, mission, values and culture. It identifies a code of conduct and provides a set of principles for dealing with poor behaviour, avoiding doubt or debate and removing personal choice (from the manager or coach, for example) in favour of the club way.

It's important to start with a clear vision and strategy, so your leadership may need to spend time on that first. You then need a club culture that links all the teams or sections.

CONSIDER:

- Who are the key people in the club that could be culture carriers?
- If you had up to five principles for your club on a poster, what would they be?

10
Partnerships

I f you turn up to watch certain grassroots sports clubs play, you will be greeted by a vision of sponsored boards, kits littered with business logos across every inch and a match day brochure that might have a page dedicated to local business sponsors. How have they achieved this? What have they done to get these connections? Why do some clubs get more sponsorship over others? This chapter should hopefully give you a level of confidence to stick your neck out as a club and go and get the right partners.

A sponsorship is cash given in return for the sponsor's branding around the ground or on the kit. At KitKing, we get thousands of sponsorship requests every year. In a typical week, we will see several enquiries come in that say: 'We are looking for sponsors for our kit. Can KitKing sponsor us?' It's clear that these clubs do not understand what the value of sponsorship is to us and how we could get a return on our investment. As a company that sells kit, it's not likely we are going to give kit away for no cost. This approach shows confidence but is lacking in forethought.

We do, however, partner with some sports clubs that have pulled together a value-added proposal in which they bring something else to the table – those who have thought about what we might want from the partnership, not just asking for £1,000 'sponsorship'. We have several top-flight sponsorships where the club can bring value to us and vice versa. In reality, the sponsorship will take the form of a larger discount, free products or a credit note. The brands we supply might also see a strategic-level partnership with a particular club within a region or that has a demographic they are supporting. If the club has a great proposal, we will often present them to brands to aid a level of sponsorship.

I believe every club has the potential to get one large or many medium and small partnership agreements. It's about who you are asking, what you are asking for, why you are asking for it and finally, how you are asking. This chapter aims to help educate on how to build a set of partners to support the growth of your club.

What makes businesses agree to give cash sponsorship?

Businesses are more likely to agree to pay cash when there is a personal link back to the club. Either the business owner has played for the club, has children that play for it or has another form of emotional connection to the sport and club. If there isn't that connection, how do you break the ice and build a connection within the club? We will explore that later in this chapter, so let's not worry about it for now.

Let's assume we have attracted a business and they are willing to pay cash; what's in it for them? Around the world, sponsoring a club is a tax-deductible activity. So, if that company is going to have a great year, they will have a large tax bill. If staff are given bonuses and all investment into the company is covered, they will likely pay corporation tax of 19–25%.

By spending a little on your club, they will be paying the taxman a little less. The taxman is happy as the money is going back into the economy via marketing, the club is happy because they are getting funds and the company is happy as they have supported a local initiative while also reducing their tax bill.

CASE STUDY: Does more than it says on the tin

During the pandemic, consumer behaviour was volatile. We were all locked down. On top of being

---

confined at home for several months in various lockdowns, we also had glorious weather in England and were not allowed to enjoy the sunshine outside of our gardens (if we had gardens) and a daily 'Boris' walk. What did we do? We spent loads of money on home and garden improvement as we had the time to complete tasks.

Ronseal, a paint brand that specialises in fence paint, reached out to KitKing in 2021. They had had unforeseen demand due to the shift in consumer behaviour and as a result, had an abnormally high profitable year. After everything was accounted for, they wanted to give back to grassroots sports and partnered with KitKing to sponsor £50,000 worth of kits to 100 clubs. Each club received £500 worth of kit at no cost. In return, the club wore the Ronseal logo on the front of their kits.

Ronseal gained great exposure, fantastic PR and it was an amazing corporate social responsibility project. The financial play here was a reduction in corporation tax as the £50,000 was classified as marketing spend.

Sponsorship versus partnership

Imagine you are a small business. Every week you get cold calls from businesses that are trying to sell you everything from phone lines and utilities to digital marketing services. A local club contacts you in June via email (as nobody seems to pick up the phone these days), requesting sponsorship of £500 for some kits for the upcoming season in July. It's an easy one to ignore, delete, pretend it went into your junk or say 'no, thank you'.

What's wrong with this approach?

- It's impersonal.

- The business hasn't been given a lot of time to add it into the financial year's budgets.

- There is no information as to why the club wants the kit or who it's for.

- There are no details about how long the sponsorship will run for.

- There are no details about the value of the sponsorship back to the sponsor or the return on investment.

The volunteer that sent this message has wasted their time, which they could have spent doing something better for the club. Let's stop thinking about asking for sponsorship and start talking about long-term club partnerships.

What are club partnerships?

Club partnerships are where the club gives a level of value to a partner and a partner gives value back. Sometimes you get lucky, and you get cash for logos on kits or ground naming rights, but there are far more creative ways to get value from partnerships.

The most important thing to recognise, is while you can go after sponsorship, there is the potential to gain so much more value for the club if you switch your mindset to partnerships. If we want our club to be oversubscribed, we need to maximise our partnerships. This will raise our profile even further, attracting more players, more volunteers and ironically... more sponsors.

Who can your club partner with?

Start by focusing on identifying and highlighting the right partners. Create a list of potential partners by category. Nothing should be off the table – nobody is too big or small for this. Only you as a club are stopping yourselves.

Once you have completed this exercise, you will have your target list of potential partners. You may be thinking, why would a potential international/global partner want to be associated with a small grassroots club? Believe it or not, if you position the club well, get to the correct department and pitch to the right people, magic can happen. What's the worst that can happen? They will ignore you or just say no. If you don't ask, you will never know.

Corporations such as Nike receive requests from a small minority of grassroots sports clubs. They often will end up in the correct department, but the team sports division are geared up to work with companies

Sample partnership identifier table for a football club in Loughborough

	Primary schools	Secondary schools	Small-medium businesses	Large corporations	Council	Governing bodies
Local (within twenty mins drive)	School name 1	School name 1	Local car dealership	McDonald's	Borough Council	Leicestershire
	School name 2	School name 2	KitKing			
Regional (within your state/county/region)	School name 3	School name 3	Local family-run garden centre	Santander HQ in Leicester	Leicestershire County Council	Leicestershire FA
National (organisations that you are linked to but are national)	Within country tour partners?	Within country tour partners?	Pure Gym	Barclays Bank (as we bank with them)	UK Government	FA – England Football Association
International (potential partners that are on a global scale)	International country tour partners?	International country tour partners?		Swiss Air because we want to tour Switzerland		FIFA – based in Switzerland
				Nike – kit		

like KitKing for partnerships. We have seen on a number of occasions that if there is a great story to be told, they will 100% invest in the project via a partner like ourselves. Alternatively, KitKing would be happy to position a club with any partner brand if the profile of the club was good and the partnership proposal adds value to the brand.

This would be the same as the club bank recommending the club to the corporate social responsibility department at the head office, for an opportunity to partner with the bank. What if the bank doesn't want to partner with you? It's never a 'no', just a 'no, not now'. Try again next year – they might have a better year, like Ronseal.

How to identify and attract potential partners

If you followed the advice in Chapter 8, you should now have a great website, social media presence and club brochure. This will put you in a good place to start contacting potential partners.

Put yourself in the potential partners' shoes. How does your club come across? Do you look credible? If you were the potential partner, would you want to partner with your club?

Before you dive into contacting partners, think about what is high value for your club and low value for the partner? What can they partner with you on that is valuable to the club but not of value to them?

How to make a case for partnership

Let's imagine a scenario at an athletics club. The club treasurer is a qualified accountant and all the accounts are completed by her and signed off. She has had a successful promotion and now must leave the club and relocate.

The leadership team has now asked the 200 members to find a replacement treasurer, and there is nobody that has the right skills for this role. A few months pass, and a new member of the club has left another club and is happy to be the club treasurer. He is skilled in managing the books; however, he is not an accountant and as the club is a limited company there is a cost associated to filing the accounts of about £3,000. This would mean all members would need to pay about £15 more per year.

The chair and secretary have used the partnership identifier table to create a list of accountants. They want to partner with a company to have the accounts filed via them, either at a reduced rate or for free.

They visit a number of accountants. Most are not interested in the club. However, a partner in a local accountancy practice has children whose friends play at the club. He agrees to send his children to the club and look at the potential of partnering with it. He takes the club brochure and pitches to the other partners in the boardroom. The other partners jump on to their phones and laptops to research the club. Positive comments are made about the website and the social media following. It's an immediate 'yes' from all partners as they calculate the cost to them would be a few days' work for a member of staff throughout the year to file the accounts.

High value to the club, low value to the partner was achieved. The club now has a cost saving of £3,000, meaning £15 per person is saved.

Strategies for making contact with potential partners

There are a number of strategies for getting in touch with potential partners: face to face, which works well for local and regional partnerships, or if you can't meet with an organisation in person, due to distance or time, the best way to get a reaction is to write an old-school letter. Use social media to reach a surprising number of followers or create a flyer to spread the word.

1. Face-to-face contact

Try and see the potential partner face to face to build rapport and see if they are a good fit for the club. If you are happy, try to invite them to the club for a headline game or event to experience and get a feel for the club culture. Invite their children, partners and families and get them involved.

Once you have brought them into the club and they have seen its culture, it is an appropriate time to ask if they would consider a partnership. Now you have broken the ice and they see the smiles on faces around the club, you are more likely to get a 'yes'.

To see this at work, let's imagine a cricket club with two full-size pitches and a lovely pavilion. The new leadership team realise that with only twenty youth team players and no coach, they are not maximising their potential. They also recognise that the club's profile is poor and they work to improve it over a year. While that is going on, a semi-pro coach is paid an hourly rate to coach the twenty youth team players. Within thirty-six months, they have over 200 youth team players and a number of coaches as they reinvest back to training other players to coach the youth section.

The leadership team realises there is potential to increase club revenue on Friday nights during the summer. They invest in outdoor seating for parents to enjoy a drink in the sunshine, socialise and watch their children. Feedback from the parents is that they would stay longer if the children were fed.

The club contacts a barbecue supplier as part of their partnership programme. The supplier is delighted to hear from them as they have never heard from a grassroots club before, and they point them in the direction of a local dealer. The dealer sells the club a top-of-the-range grill at a heavy discount and gives a discount code to the club's members. On top of this, the dealer runs barbecue chef courses at no cost to the club. The leadership nominate two volunteer chefs to run the summer barbecues.

The chefs have a great start to the first season; however, midway through the summer, parents begin leaving as soon as the cricket sessions are completed. The leadership team ask parents for their feedback, which is as follows:

- Not happy with the quality of the meat
- Not halal
- Same menu every Friday
- Minimal veggie options

As part of the partnership identifier table, the leadership had found there is a halal store close to the club. The store owner is invited to the club and turns out to be a cricket fanatic. His children play in the back garden and he never knew there was a club only a few minutes away. Rapport is built without the store owner needing to experience the club. The chairman suggests the club would love to partner with them somehow. After a few days, the store owner comes back and wants to partner with the club to provide high-quality, organic, halal meat for the barbecue during the summer. He will provide a different type of meat every week and veggie options.

The leadership team asks parents to book their meals by the Wednesday night as this is only fair to the new partner. The club will carry on charging for food, but will advertise the local business partner near the barbecue and on the online booking form.

2. The letter

The obvious method is to write an email to a head of a company. However, it's likely that this will never get to the person you have written to as often they will have staff to respond to emails. You need to stand out from the crowd and do something different.

I've always found that a typed letter with a signature in a hand-addressed envelope with a stamp gets a good response rate. By taking this traditional approach, the odds are stacked in your favour. It's likely that the letter will reach the intended person. Once that target person has been reached and the letter has been read, it's likely you will get a written response.

One club that has been actively using this technique is Beeston Hockey Club. They have identified and reached out to companies that are related to them. They have also identified local businessmen and entrepreneurs, eg Paul Smith (the global fashion icon) and the bank they previously worked with, who potentially could support them.

Here is a real-life example of a letter from Beeston to the CEO of their bank, which strikes all the right notes.

> Dear _____,
>
> I'm writing to you from Beeston Hockey Club in Nottingham. You may not be aware of the journey the club and [name of bank] have been on together over the past sixteen years.
>
> Beeston Hockey Club are one of the leading hockey clubs in Europe and have produced a wealth of Great Britain hockey players. In the 2016 Rio Olympic Games, ten of the men's and women's hockey players were current or previous members of our club. Hollie Webb, who scored the winning goal for Great Britain in the gold medal match, was also a Beeston player.
>
> The club has successfully integrated high-performance sport with an inclusive family-oriented approach, which caters for all. Enclosed with this letter is a booklet which we call our 'Aspirations document'; within it you will find detailed information about what the club has achieved and what it hopes to achieve in the future.
>
> In 2001, we received £2.1m of funding from the English Institute of Sport to develop the clubhouse and build two and a half artificial

hockey pitches. At the time, we were £400k short on the project costs, which was largely raised through a commercial mortgage with [name of bank].

All the pitches were resurfaced between 2012 and 2016. [Name of bank] have continued to support us with a commercial loan to facilitate these projects.

We have built a network of local businesses across Nottingham to support our high-performance players. We hold all our sponsors and partners in the highest regard, but [name of bank] has a special place in our hearts, because without it the club, the facility and the athletes it has produced would not be here. [Name of bank] have won an Olympic Gold medal.

There is a story here which champions [name of bank] in the sporting community outside of London. We would love to be wearing the [name of bank] logo with pride on the front of our men's and ladies' shirts.

I wondered if you would be interested in supporting the club further and being at the centre of our endeavour to grow the sport in the UK?

I look forward to hearing from you soon.

Yours sincerely,
David Griffiths
Beeston Hockey Club

Both the bank and Paul Smith kindly declined the opportunity to partner with the club, by responding to the letters they received; however, I'm certain if the opportunity did come for some level of support in the future, the seed has been planted by Beeston's letter. If they continue to write letters like that, they will get results. I wonder how many other clubs have had the courage to do that?

3. Start your search within the club

There is a theory of six degrees of separation, which states that all humans are connected within six steps. Let's have a think about how many people might be on your personal social media channel. We are going to focus on one channel to work through what this might look like.

On average, every person has 300 Facebook friends. Let's assume there are 200 adult players in your club and 100 kids, which means in theory 200 parents. 400 adults are associated with the club. Therefore 400 adults × 300 social media friends would mean an immediate reach of 120,000 people.

Obviously, there will be a little crossover as some people might have the same friends, but in theory the club has a minimum reach of 120,000 people. Within this reach, with the right messaging and campaign, you can find local partners for your club.

How can you calculate your reach as a club? The best social media channels are Instagram, Facebook and LinkedIn. First up, estimate your reach. Create a simple Google doc that can be shared with members.

An example template to calculate your club's social media reach

Player name	Facebook	Instagram	LinkedIn	Total
Player 1	300	150	200	650
Player 2	300	150	200	650
Player 3	300	150	200	650
Player 4	300	150	200	650
Player 5	300	150	200	650
Player 6	300	150	200	650
Player 7	300	150	200	650
Total	2100	1050	1400	4550

By collecting this data, it won't be long before you can calculate the club's reach through that first degree of separation. The example shows that just seven players may have a combined reach of 4,550.

Once the document is completed, make sure all the club's stakeholders realise they need to follow the club's pages and posts and actively share them. You will be surprised by what you can achieve just from within the club.

4. Go old-school with a flyer

Digital marketing is obviously the new way of marketing. However, it's also good to consider a paper flyer to complement the digital campaign. Having a flyer designed professionally is quite inexpensive if you use the websites Peopleperhour and Fiverr, or you can design it yourself with websites such as Canva (see Chapter 8).

Once the flyers have been printed, you could get older squads to hand them around in areas such as local business parks (with parents' consent if they are under eighteen). Going together and speaking to business owners as a group in unified kit will have a great impact; it's also a fantastic teambuilding task. Get the squad to research and execute the project in small groups.

Summary

This chapter gives you strategies for attracting partners who can support the growth of your club. It is a two-way relationship in which you need to bring something to the table and offer value in return for the partner's investment.

Don't overlook the connections that your membership might lead you to and make sure your profile work has been done, because the first thing prospective partners will do is Google you.

CONSIDER:

- What does your club have to offer a potential partner?
- How could you make your approaches to partners stand out?

11
Place

A stable location in which to play and train is a major factor in the success of a club. Having a home for the club to play and train will have an impact on its most important stakeholders, the players and coaches. Grassroots clubs either own their own place to play or they rent or hire a pitch or court. Either way, premises come at a huge cost to the club.

There are four clear phases of a club's development with regards to a place to play:

1. Start-up

2. Growth phase

3. Purchasing a facility

4. Getting a revenue stream from your facility

It's great for clubs to aim for phase four – where a club owns and maintains their facility, possibly with a partner. This is achievable, although it might seem a long way off. We'll investigate each phase in this chapter, but first, let's think about why place is so important.

What's it like to play on a poor facility?

I grew up playing football with my brother for a local team in Essex. It was filled with lads from our part of Chelmsford, alongside my Scout group. Coach Arnold led the team and organised the games and training.

I was good with my hands and could kick the ball quite accurately over a long distance, so Arnold coached me to be the team goalkeeper. My brother was rapid and played upfront. This was in a pre-digital era, and Arnold would phone every member of the team on a Thursday night to tell them if they were selected for that Saturday.

We were not part of a formal club and therefore didn't have a regular place to play, so Arnold would hire a pitch from the local council in Chelmsford. We would turn up with a feeling of dread as to the state of the pitch. It didn't drain properly, so if it had rained I would have to stand ankle deep in a large puddle. If it was dry, the goal mouth, which was completely worn out, would be about 30cm lower than it should be, therefore I was not able to get anywhere close to the crossbar. The pitch was awful to play on as it wasn't maintained.

The outfield was filled either with puddles or dents. If it wasn't wet, we would get a nice little present of dog poo left on the pitch. I remember my brother would slip and slide around the field trying to tackle or run with the ball and landing on dog mess.

It was awful to play on, let alone stand in goal, and it did nothing for our football. Both of us, and our mates, loved the game – that love saw us through season after season – but we hated the playing experience. We lost most games at home and won most of our games away. We were a talented bunch, but a feeling of dread built up before home fixtures, especially if the weather was awful in the days before.

After games, we were caked in mud and the changing room facilities were awful. My mum would make us remove our muddy shoes and clothes and put on dry clothes in the car park before we were taken home for a bath. Thirty-odd years later, we still talk about the wind and rain in the car park and our dread of playing at home.

Things can only get better

Fast forward thirty years and the UK government,[33] alongside governments around the world, have created opportunities to invest in club sports facilities, from clubhouses through to pitches. Alongside this investment, innovation in drainage on grass pitches has meant that the ground is less likely to be water-logged, giving a better playing experience. Other innovations include artificial pitches such as rubber crumb, which not only removes the cost of drainage but also reduces the overall maintenance time, effort and resources (no grass to cut). Overall, grassroots sports are becoming a better experience.

However, more and more clubs are struggling to find playing spaces. Many of the pitches I played on with my brother have disappeared under housing estates and have never been replaced. Start-up clubs or those looking to expand are most likely to have difficulty finding places to play.

There are many reasons to fast-track a home venue:

- To create a community hub for your club and the wider community.

- Having a home venue gives a psychological advantage to your teams.

- It doubles up as a training venue, ie you train where you play.

- If owned or part-owned, it becomes an asset to the club.

- It generates additional income for the club.

- There are advantageous social aspects for post-training or games if the clubhouse is close to the playing venue.

Phase 1: Start-up

Within the start-up phase, the priority of the club should be its people: getting the coaches in place, attracting and electing the leadership group and volunteers, and recruiting players to regularly turn up and have fun. The place to play needs to be non-committal. Great venues could be hired from local schools and universities, other clubs or local council pitches and courts.

I've seen and been part of some clubs growing out of this phase within three to four months with more players than their initial facility can hold. Others can take some time to move into phase two. In inner city locations, it may not be possible for a club to move into phase two. Space is at premium and private land-owners are likely to develop green space into commercial or residential space. Sports halls and pitches are not the most lucrative use of space.

Phase 2: Growth phase

The big question now is who you can partner with to give you the access you want – or some of it.

Teams within amateur sports clubs will have one, maybe two, training sessions per week and a fixture at the weekend. Every team will want to train and play at the same time on the same days. Therefore, as a start-up club or expansion team, compromises will have to be made, but this should not stop you from training or playing. At some venues, clubs will start training at 9pm or 10pm as this is the only slot they can get.

Let's start by identifying who potential facility owners could be:

- Existing clubs that may lack leadership or direction
- Schools and universities that have spaces not in use during evenings and weekends
- Local government or council-run facilities
- Private facilities

The key is to find facilities already built but not in use at the time of day you are wanting to use them.

The best way to find a partner is to identify common areas of 'pain'.

CASE STUDY: Working together to better facilities

Hatch Warren Tigers Netball Club in Basingstoke initially started out hiring a local school playground during spring 2021, during the Covid pandemic, when there were strict restrictions regarding playing sports indoors. Playing outdoors was not a problem during that summer – the light and weather were good – but it was clear that a problem would occur during the autumn and winter months.

After a few months, the club entered into discussions with the school. They realised that the school and club both wanted floodlights. The school was not eligible for any support for floodlights, while the Tigers didn't own the facility but potentially could access funds to get the lights installed.

The club and school worked in partnership and came up with an agreement to benefit both parties. The club would raise the funds to pay for the floodlights and in return they would receive free hire of the facility to the value of the floodlights. Win-win all round.

Phase 3: Purchasing a facility

Some might say it's impossible today to purchase land for sports. Incorrect. There are plenty of examples, even recently, of clubs purchasing land.

First and foremost, you need a group of volunteers with entrepreneurial spirit and flair and a leadership team with a 'can do' attitude. It's not likely the club will get a loan to purchase a ground or clubhouse, so there are only a few options:

- Raise funds organically with entrepreneurial ventures

- Gain financial support via an alternative source of funding

- Sell club assets (eg current land) and use funds to purchase new upgraded land/facility

Raising funds organically is tough, but I have highlighted a few ventures throughout the book, an example being the Sileby Town Fireworks Night case study in Chapter 8. Holding an annual event that raises the profile of the club as well as funds is a magic formula. Alternatively, there are several other options available to raise funds for your club.

Crowdfunding

There are many online platforms for you to use to raise funds. Most take 5% + VAT, which is currently 20%, meaning 6% of your funds go towards the platform.

Most also work on you setting a financial target to achieve; if you do not achieve your financial target then the 6% is not taken. This is known as a 'no success, no fee' basis.

The most important point about crowdfunding is that you and your leadership team will still need to promote and run events to raise money. You will have to graft to raise your profile. The wider the reach and the better your campaign story, the more likely you are to be successful.

Equity

Only clubs structured as companies limited by shares, or societies registered with the Financial Conduct Authority and with the right clauses in their constitutions, can issue equity. With the right financial guidance, clubs with the right legal structure can sell shares to investors and club members. The shareholders have the rights and ownership of the club. We hear about this in the Premier League when a new high-profile owner buys the shares of a club. If you have the right structure, grassroots clubs can do the same but increase the volume of shares to accommodate more funding.

Finance

Depending on club structure and assets, your club may be eligible for various financial products. Options may include:

- **Debt finance:** A loan with repayments plus interest, potentially from non-banking sources.

- **Mainstream finance:** A loan with repayments plus interest, from banks and building societies.

- **Social finance:** Specialist lenders who have a focus on the social impact of their lending alongside a financial return.

- **Angel investors:** Usually in the form of loans for sports clubs. Loans may have a level of collateral (for example, the assets the club owns). The more assets are used as collateral, the lower the interest rates. Angel investors in business terms will lend money in exchange for business equity. Sports clubs might not find this acceptable.

- **Peer-to-peer funding:** Funds raised from members, users or third parties. Loan period and interest is set at the point of funding.

Gift Aid

Gift Aid is a UK government scheme that allows charities and community amateur sports clubs to claim 25p on every £1 raised. There are other criteria for donations over £100. In theory, Gift Aid could add 25% to the value of the funds raised by the club.

Grants

Grants are funds that are non-refundable, ie they are 'gifted' to the organisation. Most grants come in two forms:

1. Revenue grants to help you run activities

2. Capital grants to help subsidise capital expenditure

There is plenty of money out there, but you have to be smart about finding it, and then position your club to be eligible. Be prepared to spend quite some time filling out form after form.

There may be regional grants available that are unique to your location – examples being renewal energy grants or potential funds that have been given to local government or commercial neighbours.

CASE STUDY: Fulfilling a vision to secure a home

Ashby Ivanhoe FC, founded in 1948, is a typical grassroots football club in Leicestershire. Until 2012 they were based at Hood Park in Ashby-de-la-Zouch, a local council-owned pitch, which they hired on an ad hoc basis before they moved to the NFU Sports Ground. In summer 2018, six seasons later, they were shocked to find out their landlord had gone into administration. The land they rented and played on, alongside the clubhouse, was up for sale.

The club had two options:

1. Do nothing and risk being evicted by a new owner
2. Buy the land and protect their future

The leadership group of the club decided they wanted to protect their future. What comes next is what I absolutely love about grassroots sports and the power of volunteering: a vision was created and achieved by the leadership group.

The club worked out they needed a whopping £1.3m to purchase the land and build on it. They broke it down into two phases:

1. Buy the land
2. Build the facilities and create a community hub

They recognised that they might be able to widen their funding eligibility if they changed their status to a Community Interest Club. By doing this, they would engage the wider community and the project would be open to not just football players and coaches; the clubhouse could be used by the community.

The project to raise the money started quickly, and on 30 April 2020, during the pandemic, the club exchanged contracts to buy the NFU Sports Ground for a price of £375,000 with a completion date of 1 December 2020.

Phase 4: Getting a revenue stream from your facility

Once you own your own clubhouse and playing pitches or courts, they are most definitely going to be your club's biggest assets. Like with any building and grounds, they require maintenance and general upkeep. Assets grow in value, but many sports clubs do not sweat the asset as much as possible and therefore do not have a source of regular income. When it comes to maintenance costs, they have a shortfall.

How to maximise your clubhouse

A simple exercise to work out the time the clubhouse is not being used should highlight when the asset could be used to generate income. Each club has a unique selling point. Does yours have a beautiful view that could be great for a wedding venue? Great car parking? Space for a large party?

Here are a few ideas for generating rental income from your club to kickstart your thinking:

- Evening party venue
- Weekend wedding venue
- Rent to a nursery, Monday–Friday 8.30am–4pm
- Summer sports camps
- Hire the ground out to the same sport, eg a male-only football club hires out to a female club
- Hire the ground out to another sport, eg a cricket club hires the ground to a football club during the winter
- Subscription to use club gym
- Office space

The more creative you are, the more likely you are to maximise the club's assets.

One area that is yet to be fully exploited is the rise of small companies and those that work from home or remotely. Sports clubs could potentially allow freelancers and small companies to use their facility during normal office hours. High-speed broadband might already be installed so there are no additional costs. Remote workers or small start-ups would pay to have a venue that is away from home with a stunning view and amenities, which could command a healthy passive income for the club.

Summary

This chapter explains how to solve the ever-present problem of pitches and premises: renting, buying and maintenance. It helps if you have an entrepreneurial spirit and a long-term plan.

CONSIDER:

- If you need to raise money to buy, what route could you take?
- If you're renting, where else can you try?

12
People

O ur fifth and final P is people; arguably the most important P, as a club without people is nothing. People are the oxygen of any club: they play, support and run the organisation.

CONSIDER:

- How do we get enough people?
- How do we identify people to take on volunteer roles?
- How do we encourage them to give up their time?
- How do we say thank you to volunteers?
- How do we make sure the leadership group are effective in using their time?

Sports clubs are built on the back of people giving up their time. When I was growing up in the early 1990s, sports clubs were quite close to working men's clubs. Men would go to work, pop home for their dinner and come to their local sports club until late into the night. It would almost feel as though they spent more time there than at home.

At my club, Old Chelmsfordians, the volunteer men would be at the club most evenings, if not every evening. (The most the mums did was drop off us players and pick us up from games and training.) Thankfully, a number of these older gents recognised my sporting talent. They protected me from potential harm and nurtured my talent by coaching and educating me in sport. The culture and values were not written but one person had a huge influence in my outlook towards sport. Chris Flint was my first coach. He wore multiple hats at the club: he sat on the committee, he often was the groundsman and he could be found behind the bar. At some point, he became chairman of the cricket section then president of the overall club.

Chris taught my squad about the game of cricket, but also how to become respectable young men in society. He taught me about fair play, volunteering and all the good things sports can bring to young people. The club was an extension of his family life; his sons were a little older than me and also played there. Under his guidance, I got the opportunity to play in the 1st XI at the age of fourteen with my first five-wicket haul coming that season. My first hundred came the season after.

I was the only non-white kid in the club. This would have been a problem in other clubs, but in this club I was accepted and looked after. My race wasn't a thing, but it became a thing when I played against certain other clubs. Chris and the leadership team created a culture of acceptance. I felt welcome, I felt at home. Thank you, Chris.

People like Chris now seem few and far between, but your club will also have its stars and you can certainly make the most of them.

How to attract good people

The leadership team, the players and all stakeholders need to work in harmony. Culture and philosophy need to be bought into by the club top down. Coaching, coach development and player development has to be a high priority of the leadership team.

How do you recruit and retain people who are the backbone of the club? Here are my top three tips for managing volunteers:

1. Provide high-quality coaching and coaching support (for managers/equipment/admin)

2. Create clear roles within the leadership group, alongside a set vision

3. Maximise volunteer time to support on-field activities, making use of technology to reduce admin where possible

Providing high-quality coaching

Coaches are the bedrock of a successful sports club. Great coaches that are aligned with club philosophy will bring players back, week after week. Poor or no coaches result in players leaving, grumbling or being apathetic.

Coaching is like driving a car: it looks easy until you get in front of the steering wheel and crunch the clutch. It's a skill that needs to be learnt and developed over time. Different sports have different coaching accreditations and it's good practice to have coaches get them. An unqualified and inexperienced coach can lead to a bunch of kids running around not listening and unhappy parents. Volunteer coaches need development and feedback in order to improve.

It is the leadership team's responsibility to provide guidance for the coaches on their role: engagement/fun versus development versus performance. I've coached since I was eighteen and find it rewarding – far more rewarding if you know what results you're looking for. I've now completed the ECB high-performance L3 coaching award for performance-based coaching.

Clubs need to recognise that volunteer coaches have a limited shelf life, as work, family or other pressures might impact their ability to commit. Clubs therefore need to make sure there is a pipeline of coaches being developed at different stages, so if someone leaves there is another coach ready to step in.

Sports governing bodies around the world will have courses for everything, from young helpers through to elite international coaches. If your governing body doesn't, it's likely they will recommend an accreditation in another country.

Clubs need to make sure there is budget set aside for coach development every year. This cost is an ongoing investment in the development of the club. Not everyone will be a good coach, nor will they continue coaching.

Volunteer coaches are also only as good as the management support around them. It's worthwhile appointing a manager alongside a coach to take away the administration side of coaching, eg team selection announcements, so the coach can focus on coaching. I've always found that a team manager that had nothing to do with the sport, with minimal knowledge, is often the best, because they won't want to get involved in coaching and cross paths with the coach.

A good selection of equipment will also make sure training is as effective as possible, and gives coaches options for interesting training sessions. Clubs will

GRASSROOTS TO GREATNESS

need to recognise that equipment will be broken, lost or stolen, or become defunct with wear and tear. Alongside coach development, this is an ongoing cost and there needs to be an annual budget for it. A post-season stock take of equipment will tell you what is needed. At the pre-season stage, make sure there is a document that has made it clear what equipment there is and in which area of the club. The worst culprits are balls and bibs – no matter how many you buy, you will always be short.

Creating clear roles within the leadership group

Most non-professional sports clubs are made up of volunteer parents and those that have a passion for the club. This means that the leadership of the club will be made up of those that really care. This becomes a double-edged sword, as emotions take over from rational decision making. It's therefore important for the leadership team to have clearly defined roles and a constitution that guides them through decision making.

Here are the roles that you need to consider for your leadership team:

Club president or chair

Typically the most senior person on the committee with overall responsibility for the running of the club

202

and its strategic direction. They represent the club in external matters and set the tone for the club's culture and values. If the club has both a president and a chair, the president is likely to be a figurehead and the chair the operational lead. The chair generally has the deciding vote.

Key skills:

- Strong communicator

- Well known and respected within the club

- Strategic thinker and good delegator

- Experienced in chairing meetings and making decisions

- Ability to set a vision and inspire the whole organisation to fulfil the vision

Secretary

In its simplest form, the secretary's role is to give admin support to the chair. As the club grows, the secretary might delegate administration but is primarily responsible for making sure it is done and kept in good order. A good example is making sure committee meetings and annual general meetings are minuted.

The role includes record-keeping, communicating within the club, official correspondence, maintenance of membership records, scheduling meetings and ensuring compliance with club policies and regulations. The club secretary plays a crucial and time-consuming role in ensuring effective communication and coordination within the organisation.

Key skills:

- Strong administration skills, minute taking and written communication
- High levels of attention to detail and organisation
- Deadline driven

Treasurer

The treasurer is responsible for the financial health of the club, overseeing the income and expenditure. Annual budgets and financial health checks sit within this role. The treasurer works with the chair to make sure the club is financially stable. With a vision set by the chair, the treasurer will work towards budgeting for any large capital expenses like upgrading the clubhouse or improving pitches. The treasurer can also have an entrepreneurial flair and take the lead in raising funds for the club.

The club is essentially a small business, so anyone that has experience in accounts, runs a small business or manages money in their day job is a great fit for this role.

Key skills:

- Trustworthiness and transparency
- Attention to detail
- Basic understanding of profit and loss/cashflow statements, ideally with a finance/accounting background
- Can have entrepreneurial flair
- Good stakeholder management
- Will have to stand up to the temptations to overspend

Communications officer

This role, slightly different to the secretary, is starting to emerge within committees. As we are all communicating in various ways, we need to make sure the club is communicating in the way its membership wants. The communications officer would be responsible for social media posts and email newsletters.

Key skills:

- Digitally savvy and creative
- Needs to understand the club could be multi-generational and communications might need to be repeated in different formats

Coach

Coaches are responsible for the development of players. It makes sense to have input from a coach on the leadership team.

Key skills:

- Ability to build rapport with athletes, parents, other coaches, leadership team

- Ability to ask powerful questions

- Create a fun learning environment whilst also being able to be performance driven

- Strong observational skills

- Strong organisational and communication skills

Captain

The captain is the on-pitch or on-court leader. At grassroots level, the captain might also be the coach and the selector of players. Good captains also end up leading their players off the field through social activities as the squad bonds. Great captains are not only the captain of the assigned team, they are also leaders within the club.

Key skills:

- Strong leadership skills

- A great ability to connect with people through the club and assigned squad

More established clubs may have the following:

Team manager or head coach

The team manager or head coach is responsible for leading and managing a specific team (or teams) within the club. They provide guidance and support to the players, make tactical decisions, and ensure the team's overall performance and development. The team manager or head coach also liaises with other club officials, such as the chair. The coach sets the philosophy of the club alongside the leadership group.

Key skills:

- Patience and gravitas

- Excellent communication and admin skills

- Good role model with positive energy

Youth development director

In clubs with a focus on developing young athletes, a youth development director or similar title may be appointed. This individual is responsible for designing and implementing programmes that nurture the talents of young players, overseeing coaching and training and ensuring a smooth transition of players from the youth ranks to senior teams. The youth development director works alongside the head coach to make sure the philosophy of the club is carried through to the junior teams.

Key skills:

- Patience and gravitas

- Excellent communication and admin skills

- Good role model with positive energy

Marketing and public relations manager

The marketing and public relations manager is responsible for promoting the club, attracting sponsors and managing public relations. They develop marketing strategies, coordinate advertising campaigns, manage social media presence, and work to enhance the club's public image and brand awareness. These days, most of this work is done via website platforms and social media. More and more clubs are creating a separate social media role within the leadership group.

Key skills:

- Communication

- Creativity

- Written skills

- Photography / videography
- Editing skills
- Social media skills

Facilities and operations manager

In larger sports clubs with dedicated facilities, an operations manager may be appointed to oversee the day-to-day operations of the club's facilities. They ensure proper maintenance, manage bookings and rentals, coordinate events and ensure the smooth functioning of the club's physical infrastructure.

Key skills:

- Organisational skills
- Problem solving
- Gravitas, ability to engage in volunteer workforce
- Planning
- Communication

Maximise volunteer time

We are all reliant on volunteers to build our clubs, therefore know people have given up their precious time; we need to maximise it as much as possible.

People have higher demands on their time than ever before, be it work or family time. When I was younger, the men that ran my club would get home from a busy day at work, food was on the table, they ate and were straight back out to the club. Their families and wives accepted this was part of their life. This is no longer the case; times have moved on and roles and responsibilities at home are now blended, so time pressures of our volunteers are at an all-time high.

Simple examples of maximising volunteer time could be using https://otter.ai to help write up meeting minutes or running meetings on Zoom instead of face-to-face meetings. I'm a keen advocate of reducing data input as much as possible. If your club is quite large and you are selecting from a large pool of players, a selection meeting and then working out who is OK to play (or not) can be a painful weekly task. Websites such as Pitchero or apps such as Plai or Spond are a fantastic way of reducing admin for busy captains. ChatGPT and AI based software can have a huge impact on marketing, social media, finance/accounting, customer services/inbound emails and inventory management within the clubhouse.

Overall, technology can save a huge amount of time for our people, which can potentially increase their length of service to the club, increase productivity and also increase the quality of the output for the club.

Why elections are important

Most grassroots sports clubs are owned by members, while professional clubs are being bought by wealthy individuals and institutions for commercial reasons.

Member-owned clubs have a constitution or articles of association. The guardian of the constitution is the democratically elected committee or leadership team. It is their responsibility to uphold the constitution or articles of association.

The election of committee or leadership groups is important in order for the members to have the best representatives. As a grassroots club, you may think the election process is unimportant, or as a committee member you might feel obliged to stay on as there isn't anyone to take over.

Correctly running the election process of committees raises the bar of the voluntary role. If people are frustrated by the way the club is being run, they need encouragement to show ambition or challenge the existing person in the role. At Loughborough, Dr Guy Jackson encouraged me to stand for election as he could see my frustration would result in me resolving many of the club's issues.

Even in professional clubs that have a democratic leadership, some run campaigns to rival national government campaigns. The best examples of this would be Real Madrid or Barcelona. Both clubs' presidential campaigns are huge affairs with the role being taken extremely seriously by all stakeholders within the club. By having a level of importance on the role and creating competition for places, the candidates that are finally elected are naturally the best.

How to have effective committee or leadership group meetings

Nobody wants to give up their time for badly run meetings and for a club to not be moving forward.

Top tips for running successful meetings

1. Make sure meetings are regular – create a habit.

2. Remind everyone of the three- to five-year objectives and BHAGs, every meeting.

3. Remind everyone of the club's philosophy.

4. Set an agenda. Ask the group for input and agenda items and publish these three to four days in advance. Identify clear objectives and outputs for each meeting.

5. Actively make sure everyone has their points heard.

6. Ensure the meetings stick to the agenda (over-talkers can take the meeting off course).

7. Foster a culture of respectful and constructive debate, where differing viewpoints can be expressed, discussed and evaluated to reach informed decisions.

8. Clearly define action items, including responsibilities, deadlines and follow-up mechanisms, to ensure progress is made between meetings.

What to avoid in a leadership or committee meeting

1. Dominating the discussion. Make sure you allow others to be heard; keep an eye on how much you talk compared to others.

2. Blaming or personal attacks.

3. Distractions, such as phone use. Meetings can take a lot longer if people are not listening.

4. Allowing conversations to move off the agenda.

5. Being rushed into making decisions. Make sure you have all the facts before decisions are made.

6. Ignoring non-verbal cues. Make sure you are keeping an eye on everyone. They will tell you with their body language if they are not engaged.

These points will make your committee meetings more efficient, inclusive and productive, leading to better decision making, outcomes and, hopefully, fun.

Wrexham: the ultimate grassroots to greatness story

Wrexham AFC has had a chequered past – a rich history that dates back to 1864. The club plays at the Racecourse Ground, which happens to be the world's oldest international football ground. It faced bankruptcy in 1988 but was saved by local newspaper wholesaler Pryce Griffiths stepping in as majority shareholder.

More recent troubles started in 2002 when the club was purchased by individuals who were interested in its most valuable asset, the Racecourse Ground, rather than success on-pitch. Within only twenty-four months, the club faced an unprecedented level of financial problems and unpaid taxes meant that it could lose the ground.

In June 2004, the Wrexham Supporters Trust (WST) stepped in. Similar to the Portsmouth FC fans (see Chapter 4), they raised the required funds and ownership of the club changed to them. The entire process took until 2005. That season, the players won the FA League Trophy, giving fans something to feel positive about.

The WST moved away from ownership a few years later, but with more problems stepped back in again in 2011. During this time, the club had slipped down the football pyramid through to the National League (Step 6). This level of football can be described as top of grassroots and aspiring professional clubs.

In May 2020, during the pandemic, the WST started to consider getting help raising funds in order to get external investment. By November 2020, the club had a Zoom call with Hollywood A-listers Ryan Reynolds and Rob McElhenney. This was a pitch by Rob and Ryan to the WST – the start of a story that was to change the future of the club and the community within Wrexham.

Their pitch to the WST board can be framed within the five Ps.

Profile

With Rob and Ryan having a combined social media following of over fifty million, just on Instagram, by their association the club's profile would naturally increase. Rob and Ryan pitched the concept of creating content that could be sold to streaming services of a 'grassroots to greatness story'. This would raise the profile and bring in a revenue stream not seen at this level of football.

Partnerships

By raising the profile of the club, Ryan and Rob shared the belief that sponsors would want to be associated with it. Sponsorship agreements on a global and local level would become highly attractive.

As Ryan Reynolds also fully owns or has a stake in a number of businesses, there would be a symbiotic relationship between the club, Ryan, and his other business interests, for example Aviation American Gin.

Place

Rob and Ryan researched the club prior to their pitch, reportedly watching footage as far back as the 1970s. They understood the importance of the Racecourse Ground and the role it plays for the club, the community and the nation of Wales. They vowed to invest in the infrastructure and committed to spending £2m. They also promised the fans that the club would not be renamed, relocated or rebranded.

By the end of 2023, Rob and Ryan had invested far more than the £2m originally promised. They supported the club's growth and saw it promoted into the EFL. The promise they made regarding not relocating the ground has been confirmed; however, the Racecourse Ground has been renamed the STōK Cae Ras, thanks to a coffee sponsorship deal.

Philosophy

Rob, Ryan and the leadership team they created had little to no on-field experience. They recruited men's and women's coaches with playing philosophies they agreed with. Most importantly, as you can see from the second season of the docuseries *Welcome to Wrexham*,[34] they allow the coaches to do their jobs. They are understanding and supportive when a plan doesn't come to fruition, and passionate and congratulatory when winning. They have created a leadership with people who have bought into their vision and a level of experience.

As a grassroots club, you may not have the luxury of picking and choosing your leadership team. Which is more important: buying into the vision or having the experience? In my humble opinion, having a group of people buying into a vision is absolutely the preferred option.

People

If you haven't seen *Welcome to Wrexham*, I urge you to watch it. The second series gives an insight into the Wrexham leadership team's relationship with the people of Wrexham. We see a spotlight being shone on fans, local businesses, local pubs, staff, coaches, the men's team, the women's team and the families that support them. All the people have bought into the club's vision. This can be seen in abundance in the docuseries.

The individual stakeholders are clear on their roles, which they are allowed to execute. The overall mission statement, which you can read at www.wrexhamafc.

co.uk/the-club/mission-statement, is clear and transparent and is referred to by stakeholders.

All in all, Wrexham AFC's story tells you everything you need to know.

Summary

This chapter tells you how to develop and support coaches and other volunteers, and how to recruit an effective leadership team and maximise its time.

CONSIDER:

- Are you doing everything you can to develop your people?
- Have you taken care of your pipeline?

Conclusion

My grassroots sports journey and career within the sports industry has led me to write this book. The formulas and theories are based on a combination of experiences and rudimentary data collection.

A new era of top-level female sport

We are entering into a new era of team sports – a clear shift on a global scale. My daughters cannot comprehend that their mother and grandmothers were not allowed to play most team sports. From 1921 to 1970, women's football was banned in England by the FA. It has taken from 1970 until the last ten years for equality in sport to come to the forefront of governing bodies around the world.

Why? Well there has been far too much to sort out within the men's game. We are now at a point of commercial maturity of the men's game in almost every sport, meaning there is a new market of female fans to consume sport. Their requirements are unknown.

CONSIDER:

- How will women and girls consume and participate in team sport?
- How might they want to play sport in a different way?
- Do women get different types of injuries to men?
- Do women continue to play after childbirth?
- Are we going to see sponsorship rights dedicated to men's and women's teams and leagues?

We do not have enough grassroots female population or eyeballs globally yet for us to truly understand the answers to these questions.

There is no doubt that the rise of top-level female sport will inspire the next generation of girls to play grassroots sports. We therefore are going to double our playing population as more clubs open up to females. Clubs that embrace this change and focus on the five Ps will capitalise on this shift. Those that don't are likely to disappear, merge with other clubs or be acquired. We are also going to see the rise of female-only clubs. Already, we are seeing many male clubs that want to have a female section but do not have the capacity to manage. Either start-up clubs are emerging or clubs affiliated to a men's section are being created.

What might the future look like?

Successful grassroots clubs are currently bulging at the seams. With more focus put on the women's game, I predict the rise of female-only clubs. We will no doubt have mixed clubs, but more and more grass-roots clubs are struggling to manage without paid staff. This trend has been emerging over the past few years and is not likely to stop. In late 2023 the Women's Super League and Championship announced that it will break away from the English FA. This new guardian of the top tier of the women's league could set a trend for the future. Could grassroots women's team sports follow this trend?

Will your club be part of this and other changes to come?

You now know how to run a sports club that serves all of your community, with a smooth pathway for new talent and a plan for the next generation. You know how to achieve a clear vision and a culture that everyone is happy to buy into, and a leadership team that pulls together and uses its time well.

You have applied the C+L+U=B framework so you can see the areas where you need to improve and have reflected on the five Ps (profile, philosophy, partnerships, place and people). This will give your leadership team discussion points for committee meetings, whether you're sorting out your branding or thinking about raising money for state-of-the-art premises.

Because you've got to do the work, but I'm here to support you with my club resources.

I look forward to hearing your stories of growth, and on- and off-field success.

Notes

1 All Blacks, 'About The Team', www.allblacks.com/teams/all-blacks, accessed 17 April 2024

2 J Kerr, *Legacy: What the All Blacks can teach us about the business of life* (Constable & Robinson, 2013)

3 S Sinek, *Start With Why: How great leaders inspire everyone to take action* (Portfolio, 2009)

4 J Kerr, *Legacy: What the All Blacks can teach us about the business of life* (Constable & Robinson, 2013)

5 Ibid

6 A Elberse, 'Ferguson's Formula', *Harvard Business Review* (October 2013), https://hbr.org/2013/10/fergusons-formula, accessed 17 April 2024

7 Ibid

8   Ibid
9   Ibid
10 Ibid
11 Ibid
12 Ibid
13 Ibid
14 Ibid
15 Ibid
16 Ibid
17 Oxford University Press, *social capital*, Oxford Learner's Dictionaries [online], www.oxfordlearnersdictionaries.com/definition/english/social-capital?q=social+capital, accessed 24 February 2024
18 EFL, *Measuring the Impact of EFL Clubs in the Community: 2019–2022 National Report*, www.efl.com/community/our-impact, accessed 8 November 2024
19 Tranmere Rovers, 'Tranmere Rovers in the Community – Tackling Loneliness Together' (3 August 2020), https://tranmererovers.co.uk/news/2020/august/tranmere-rovers-in-the-community---tackling-loneliness-together, accessed 24 February 2024
20 R Simpson, 'Darlington FC Launches Buddy Scheme', *The Quakers* (6 April 2020), https://darlingtonfc.co.uk/news/darlington-fc-launches-buddy-scheme, accessed 24 February 2024
21 Stevenage FC, 'Stevenage FC Coronavirus Community Careline', www.stevenagefc.com/more/community-careline, accessed 24 February 2024

22 Stockport County FC, 'County donate £75,000 to Stockport NHS Trust', https://stockportcounty. com/county-donate-75000-to-stockport-nhs-trust, accessed 24 February 2024

23 Communities, 'Coronavirus: Clubs help tackle social isolation', Premier League (10 May 2020), www.premierleague.com/news/1648458, accessed 27 November 2024

24 K Lewin, R Lippitt and RK White, 'Patterns of aggressive behavior in experimentally created "social climates"', *The Journal of Social Psychology*, 10 (1939), 271–299, https://doi.org/1 0.1080/00224545.1939.9713366

25 M Smith and S Figgins, 'Five Ways Jürgen Klopp's Leadership Style Helped Liverpool to the Top', *The Conversation* (26 June 2020), www. nextgov.com/ideas/2020/06/five-ways-jurgen-klopps-leadership-style-helped-liverpool-top/166482, accessed 26 February 2024

26 UNESCO, 'International Charter of Physical Education, Physical Activity and Sport' (6 October 2022), www.unesco.org/en/sport-and-anti-doping/international-charter-sport, accessed 26 February 2024

27 Sky Sports Cricket (@SkyCricket) 'You are a very special talent…' (26 December 2019), https://twitter.com/SkyCricket/status/1210279686082846722, accessed 26 February 2024

28 James Anderson (@jimmy9) 'A proud day receiving my 150th test cap…' (26 December

2019), https://twitter.com/jimmy9/
status/1210288101890936838, accessed 26
February 2024

29 M Bass-Krueger 'Everything to know
about the history of the blazer', *Vogue* (28
November 2019), www.vogue.com.au/
fashion/trends/everything-to-know-about-
the-history-of-the-blazer/image-gallery/
dd07db6a3e45b3cbaff5851eb1b20398, accessed
22 November 2024

30 'Our History', Marylebone Cricket Club (no
date), www.lords.org/mcc/the-club/our-
history, accessed 22 November 2024

31 The FA, 'What is the England DNA' (24
November 2020), https://help.thefa.com/
support/solutions/articles/7000042843-what-is-
the-england-dna-, accessed 27 February 2024

32 FC Barcelona, '50 years of "more than a club"'
(17 January 2018), www.fcbarcelona.com/en/
news/723765/50-years-of-more-than-a-club,
accessed 27 February 2024

33 Gov.uk, 'Multi-Sport Grassroots Facilities
Programme projects: 2022 to 2023' (20 May
2023), www.gov.uk/guidance/multi-sport-
grassroots-facilities-programme-projects-2022-
to-2023, accessed 27 February 2024

34 Boardwalk Pictures, *Welcome to Wrexham*
(streamed on Disney+, 2022–23), www.
disneyplus.com/en-gb/series/welcome-
to-wrexham/4NwOxyDF4T3A, accessed 27
February 2024

Acknowledgements

First my wife Parisha, my partner in life and business, who always challenges me to be better. Thank you for being CEO of our home and supporting me to write this book.

My mum and dad, who pushed myself and my brother to get involved in every sport – rugby, football and cricket. Thank you for taking us to all the training sessions, games and summer schools and being our taxi service.

Chris Flint, my first coach, thanks for being there for me and my friends from the age of eleven. Thank you for all your words of wisdom and patience in nurturing us, not just as sportsmen but as leaders on and off the field.

Joe Middleton, my first CEO at Canterbury of New Zealand. Thank you for giving me my first job as a graduate and giving me the opportunity to work with some of the most iconic clubs around the world in numerous sports.

Charlotte Cox, President EMEA Pentland Brands, thank you for employing me at Speedo and Pentland Brands. You were an outstanding manager, thank you for supporting all the crazy product concepts I put forward and giving me the spotlight to present them. The way we carry out partnerships today has been based on the way you taught me.

David Robinson, former President of Speedo, thank you for being the inspiring business leader. Thank you for being there on a personal and professional level.

Andy Rubin, Chairman of Pentland Brands. Thank you for creating an environment that allowed me to learn about the sporting goods industry and a world-class family-run business all whilst having fun along the way.

Finally, the team at KitKing who are awesome! Thank you for supporting me through the journey writing this book. In particular James, Sam, Victoria and Paul.

The Author

Dips landed his first volunteer role at Loughborough University when he was eighteen. At the age of twenty he was elected by the student population to the role of Vice President Finance and Commercial Services of the Students Union. The role had overall responsibility for the profit of the student union – a £9m turnover business with about 400 staff. By the time he graduated a few years later, he had won several university awards for the clubs and societies he led. The highest accolades were Club Colours for the Loughborough Students Cricket Club and the Professor Sir David Wallace Award, directly from the Vice Chancellor for services to the students and their experience at Loughborough. Whilst at university, Dips also gained his coaching badges leading him to be appointed assistant coach at the university a few years after he graduated.

During his time at university, Canterbury of New Zealand tried to employ him. Dips agreed a part-time role in his final year until he graduated, then continued for four more years in a global role. He worked with international federations, professional clubs, grassroots clubs, universities, colleges and schools around the world. He was stationed in Australia and South Africa and launched various categories around the world. His highlights were working with the Springboks during the time they lifted the World Cup in 2007 and working with Portsmouth FC when they won the FA Cup in 2008.

Following his time at Canterbury, he moved to Speedo, launching the world's first underwater MP3 player 'Speedo Aquabeat' and Speedo's automated lap counting watch 'Aquacoach'. Whilst at Speedo, was asked to be a guest lecturer at Nottingham Trent University in business, innovation and marketing, a role he still holds today.

Following his corporate career, Dips joined his wife Parisha in their family business. Since 2015 Dips has forged ahead as an entrepreneur, building, buying, financing and restructuring businesses. In 2019 Dips and Parisha acquired KitKing.co.uk, one of the

UKs largest team sports dealers, and have expanded the business to Ireland. Dips and Parisha launched KitQueen.co.uk in 2023, as they believe the female athlete and her requirements are underserved.

He is now regarded as one of the UK's leading team sports industry experts.

Today Dips works alongside Parisha and his team to bring global sports brands to clubs from grassroots through to international federations. Dips has stepped away from professional coaching, but still volunteers and coaches with his two daughters' teams.

To learn more, visit:

⊕ https://grassrootstogreatness.club